GENERAL JOSEPH BLOOMFIELD

BLOOMFIELD
[NEW JERSEY]
OLD AND NEW

*An Historical Symposium
by Several Authors*

Edited by
Joseph Fulford Folsom

HERITAGE BOOKS
2010

HERITAGE BOOKS
AN IMPRINT OF HERITAGE BOOKS, INC.

Books, CDs, and more—Worldwide

For our listing of thousands of titles see our website
at
www.HeritageBooks.com

A Facsimile Reprint
Published 2010 by
HERITAGE BOOKS, INC.
Publishing Division
100 Railroad Ave. #104
Westminster, Maryland 21157

Copyright © 1912
Bloomfield Centennial Historical Committee

— Publisher's Notice —

In reprints such as this, it is often not possible to remove blemishes from the original. We feel the contents of this book warrant its reissue despite these blemishes and hope you will agree and read it with pleasure.

International Standard Book Numbers
Paperbound: 978-0-7884-3009-1
Clothbound: 978-0-7884-7493-4

CONTENTS

	Page
FOREWORD	7
THE BEGINNINGS. JOSEPH F. FOLSOM	11
THE "1776" PERIOD. JOSEPH F. FOLSOM	32
AFTER THE REVOLUTION. JOSEPH F. FOLSOM	43
INCORPORATION AND SUBSEQUENT GOVERNMENT. RAYMOND F. DAVIS	69
THE SCHOOLS AND SCHOOLMASTERS. WILLIAM A. BALDWIN	78
TRANSPORTATION. CHARLES C. FERGUSON	101
THE HISTORY OF THE CHURCHES. GEORGE LOUIS CURTIS	118
MUNICIPAL DEVELOPMENT. WILLIAM P. SUTPHEN	140
THE ANNALS OF STONE HOUSE PLAINS (BROOKDALE). JAMES E. BROOKS	162
AN AFTERNOON WALK. MAUD PARSONS	180

APPENDICES

BOARD OF TRADE RESOLUTION	184
ACT OF INCORPORATION (1812)	186
CENTENNIAL CELEBRATION AND COMMITTEE	188
SUB-COMMITTEES OF THE CENTENNIAL CELEBRATION	189
INDEX	191

ILLUSTRATIONS

General Joseph Bloomfield, Former Governor of New Jersey . . . . *Frontispiece*	
	Facing Page
Daniel Dodd House (1719)	18
Thomas Cadmus House	40
Joseph Davis House	48
Soldiers' and Sailors' Monument (1912) . .	68
Madame Cooke's School (1856)	84
Bloomfield High School (1912)	98
Presbyterian Church, Lecture Room and Stone Schoolhouse (1840)	120
Along the Yantecaw or Third River . .	140
Jarvie Memorial Library	167
The "Stone House" of the "Plains" . .	168
Map of Bloomfield in 1830	184

FOREWORD

THIS book, though brief, adds many facts about Bloomfield hitherto unpublished. It also brings together much scattered material previously printed. Of necessity, because of time and space limitations, it leaves out many good things already in book form. It is a contribution to the materials for a history of the town.

This historical sketch very strikingly differs from previous ventures. It is a symposium of narratives by different authors to whom special departments were assigned. What it lacks in unity it makes up in data. It is a compendium of annals rather than an essay in history. For the sake of future historical accuracy the names of the authors are prefixed to the respective articles.

The idea of preparing this volume originated in the Historical Committee appointed by the Executive Committee of the Bloomfield Board of Trade, the latter committee having been created to arrange for the celebrating of the centennial anniversary of the incorporation in 1812 of Bloomfield. The Historical Committee was constituted as follows: Benjamin Haskell, Chairman, William A. Baldwin, Secretary, Charles C. Ferguson, Rev. George L. Curtis, D.D., Rev. Joseph F. Folsom, William P. Sutphen and Raymond F. Davis. The purpose in view was a souvenir that might have historical value, and also help to conserve the spirit and sentiment of the celebration.

Many things that ought to be said are of necessity omitted. Every political, military, social and benevolent organization might furnish materials for a long chapter, but to find the room has been impossible. Much material of this kind appears in the souvenir publication of the Executive Committee, and more, let us hope, will appear when in the course of time the next history of Bloomfield shall go to press.

Those who have prepared the articles desire to acknowledge their indebtedness to previous compilers of material on Bloomfield, and to the many interested friends who have furnished information and suggestion. Previous books and general sketches on Bloomfield, all of which have been directly or indirectly helpful, are listed as follows:

"Plea for the Old Foundations," by Rev. James M. Sherwood, an historical sermon on the "Old First" Presbyterian Church of Bloomfield, with an appendix by Rev. Stephen Dodd, published by M. W. Dodd, New York, 1854.

"The Church on the Green," by Rev. Charles E. Knox, D.D., an historical sermon on the "Old First," delivered in 1896, in connection with its centennial celebration, and published by Stephen Morris Hulin, Bloomfield, 1901.

"Fiftieth Anniversary of the First Baptist Church, Bloomfield, N. J.," compiled by David G. Garabrant, an account of the exercises and the historical addresses delivered in 1901 on that occasion, and printed later by the Avil Printing Company, Philadelphia.

"Real and Ideal Bloomfield," by Stephen Morris Hulin, a copiously illustrated volume telling the story of "Church-Town, Township and Incorporated Town of To-day," published at Bloomfield, printed by Groebe-McGovern Co., Newark, 1902.

"Bloomfield Township," by Rev. Charles E. Knox, an article in Shaw's "History of Essex and Hudson Counties," published in two volumes by Everts and Peck, Philadelphia, 1884.

Four manuals, or directories, of the "Old First" church have been published, and each, with the exception of that dated 1889, contains an historical sketch of the town and church. The dates of these publications are 1835, 1860, 1889 and 1906. The last mentioned of these pamphlets contains an excellent sketch of the inception and organization of the church during the years 1794 to 1800. It was carefully prepared by Hon. Amzi Dodd, and is the best account extant of that interesting ecclesiastical period.

There have been many other sources; literary, documentary, and word of mouth. Some of the Revolutionary and other stories have appeared previously in various articles prepared by the editor of this book some years ago for the Newark *Evening News,* one of which, under the caption "Historic Bloomfield," was reprinted in the *Bloomfield Citizen,* on September 1, 1900.

The compiler of the chapter on schools expresses indebtedness to William E. Chancellor, formerly the superintendent of the local schools, and the compiler of the annals of Stone House Plains, to William Nelson of Paterson, and Lewis Cockefair of Bloomfield. Mr. Nelson's unpublished "History of Paterson and Passaic County," and the reminiscences of Mr. Cockefair were especially helpful.

The compiler of the sketches of the churches desires to thank also the various pastors for their kindness in providing the required materials.

Two other names must here be included, those of the

late John Oakes, and his still living friend, Mark W. Ball, of Newark. Many facts years ago furnished by Mr. Oakes to the writer of this foreword have been added to the various articles, particularly to those of the Revolutionary and the early nineteenth century period. The inserted map of Bloomfield in the year 1830, inscribed with the names of the residents of that period, was originally drafted by Mr. Oakes, and through the courtesy of John F. Capen prepared for this volume. Mr. Ball at the age of ninety-three is still clear in mind, and his reminiscences have been of much value.

Whatever the limitations and defects of this latest contribution to local annals, they cannot lessen our love and respect for the old town and the new town whose centennial we unite to celebrate. We may take upon our lips the lines of the poet Henry Kirke White, written to celebrate the fame of a brother poet, and apply them with equal homage to our town of the same name:

"Bloomfield, thy happy-omen'd name
    Ensures continuance to thy fame;
Both sense and truth this verdict give,
    While fields shall bloom, thy name shall live."

J. F. F.

May, 1912.

THE BEGINNINGS

By Joseph F. Folsom

ABOUT the year 1700 a sturdy race of people began to settle the region now called Bloomfield. The lay of the land was inviting. Here was a fertile plain covered with virgin forests and flanked by tillable uplands. Two small rivers, by name Second and Third, watered the region and gave promise of numerous mill sites. To clear the land, saw the timber, and break the soil was an attractive task. It suited well the type of men who undertook it. These founders labored in hope. They worked for not only themselves but for their descendants. They were not quitters. They came to stay.

These first settlers were mostly young men. They were the sons and the grandsons of the Connecticut men who, in 1666 and the years following, had landed on the bank of the Passaic River and founded the town of Newark. The boundaries of Newark extended from Elizabeth on the south to Acquackanonk on the north, with the Passaic River on one side and the Watchung Mountain on the other. The region destined to become Bloomfield was the northern section of the tract. For some years it lay for the most part an unbroken wilderness. The original Newark men knew that these outlands were securely in their possession. They had enough on their hands developing the section near their home lots by the river. Their heirs and descendants might occupy the outlands in due time. Their immediate task was big enough for one lifetime. They willingly left further conquests to the younger men.

The older men, however, did not leave the future settling of these outlands wholly to chance. There were many who with prudence and foresight reached out and secured individual possession of tracts of land they intended never personally to occupy. They might cut off the timber, and erect saw mills, or they might use available spaces for grazing their cattle; but age and community instincts held them to the village life by the Passaic. When in time their six-acre lots became inadequate to support their growing families, their sons struck out to make homes for themselves in the wilderness. The grants in this region obtained by the older men thus determined to a great extent who should be the future inhabitants of Bloomfield. The same principle, of course, operated in other outlying sections.

Another cause to have delayed somewhat the settling of this region was the vague fear of Indians which naturally clung to the early settlers. Long after Newark was settled the inhabitants kept watch and ward against possible attack. As late as 1689 a committee of safety was appointed by the town. This fear had no reference to the nearby remnants of savage tribes, but to possible incursions of warriors from beyond the Delaware. The Hackensack Indians, from whom the Newark men purchased their township, were a feeble remnant. They had once been troublesome, but on February 25, 1643, the Dutch of Manhattan had crossed the Hudson and cruelly massacred Indian men, women and children at Pavonia. Eighty souls were that bloody night set free by the command of Governor William Kieft, so that David De Vries, waiting in the governor's house in New Amsterdam, heard the shooting and the wailing on the New Jersey side, and called it butchery.

All this took place a quarter of a century before Newark was settled.

The ancestors of the young men who settled Bloomfield came from Connecticut. The first group to reach the Passaic came from the town of Milford. Then followed the Branford people, and later others from Guilford and New Haven. They were a sturdy lot of men and women, who had known privation and difficult enterprises. They had been in Indian wars, and some of the Branford group had, in 1640, attempted to form a settlement at Southampton on Long Island, but had abandoned the project and returned to Connecticut. When the opportunity to establish a new home in New Jersey presented itself they again bravely packed their goods and emigrated. Their reasons for desiring a change were mainly religious, though the economic element was not wholly absent. The Newark settlers generally desired a community in which full citizenship should be granted only to members of the church, and such communities had ceased to exist in the New Haven Colony. The Newark settlement has been characterized as the last attempt on the American continent to establish a theocracy. The principle was doubtless narrow, and could not operate permanently, but the men who held it had broad brains and plenty of backbone. They were capable of widening their intellectual horizon.

It is important to know who among this band of early settlers took up lands in the section now Bloomfield. Such knowledge, as far as it goes, helps us to understand why certain families increased in this region. In this matter we shall not consider the early settlers of Belleville, once a part of Bloomfield, or generally of Montclair, once West Bloomfield. Also we shall pass over the founders of Stone House Plains, for the reason that they will be fully considered in a later chapter.

The Crane family, which peopled the locality called Cranetown, and later West Bloomfield and Montclair, cannot be passed over. Members of this stock during almost two centuries were influential in the affairs of Bloomfield. Their common ancestor was Jasper Crane of Newark. Next to Captain Robert Treat he was the leading figure of the colony. He was a Branford man, and his name stands first on the list of those who signed the two fundamental agreements underlying the Newark government, namely church membership in order to full citizenship, and diligent maintenance of the religion professed in the Congregational church. Jasper Crane was an inveterate emigrant. He was one of the founders of the New Haven Colony in 1639. He probably was among the number who settled Branford in 1644. He made plans in 1651 to establish a colony on the Delaware River, but was prevented by the Dutch. He came to Newark in the fall of 1666, and in 1675, among other scattered properties, he secured twenty acres "at the head of a branch of the Second River." This tract was doubtless near the center of the present Montclair. Jasper died in 1681, and his will, drawn in 1678, mentions his children as John, Azariah, Jasper and Hannah. Azariah was living "at the Mountain" as early as 1715, and it is thought that he and his brother Jasper were the first settlers of that part of Bloomfield. One of the descendants of Azariah was Major Nathaniel Crane, who gave to the Bloomfield church its first bell, strongtoned enough to be heard to the mountain. He gave generously toward building the Bloomfield Academy in 1810, and left a fund for the education of young men for the ministry which is still in use. Among the five Cranes who gave liberally toward the erection of the Bloomfield "Old First" Church and the thirteen of that stock who were charter members, was Israel Crane, the famous road-builder. He was interested in many social, religious, commercial and philanthropic movements in Bloomfield.

The settlement of that part of Bloomfield formerly called Watsesson Plain, including the whole section from Watsesson Hill to the Morris Neighhorhood, was begun by the Baldwin, Davis, Dodd, Morris and Ward families. Taking as a guide the "Old Road," said to have been an ancient Indian trail to the interior, we find along the route, even as late as 1800, quite well-defined areas in which these early families had become fixed. The earliest Baldwin property lay between the "Old Road" and the Second River, and on the eastern slope of Watsesson Hill. Then came the Dodd tracts, running east and west of the road, along the course of the Second River. The Dodd influence extended to Doddtown. To the west of the road, and embracing what is now the business center of Bloomfield, was next the Ward area, running at least as far as Toney's Brook. East of the road, and opposite the Ward tract, was the Davis property, extending from the present Montgomery Street to Belleville Avenue, formerly including the Green and the church and the school properties. Above Belleville Avenue, on both sides of the road, was more of the Baldwin influence, running up to the Morris area. The Morris influence was along the Yanticaw, or Third River, in the neighborhood of Bay Lane.

Benjamin Baldwin, the weaver, was the founder ancestor of most of the Baldwins of Bloomfield. He came from Milford, Connecticut, and was in Newark in the fall of 1666, a young man aged twenty-six years. There was given him a home lot in Newark, located west of the present Washington Avenue, near Warren Street. He took up land between the Second and Third rivers, and north of the highway leading over Watsesson Hill. Among his descendants was David Baldwin, born about 1715, from whom most of the family who located near the Third River and Morris Neighborhood are descended. When David was eighty-five years old he could still drive his team to a swamp by the river and bring home a load of wood. David and his sons owned three mill sites on Third River, and most of the farms between the church and Morris Neighborhood. He was a charter member of the old church, and his wife and eight children had the same honor. The children were Zophar, David, Silas, Jesse, Ichabod, Eunice, Sarah, and Simeon. Jesse was a quartermaster in the Continental Army. It was Simeon who opposed the project to build a frame church, and vigorously declared for a permanent structure of stone. He operated a grist and fulling mill. He died September 7, 1806. Caleb Dodd Baldwin, a grandson of David, enlisted at the age of seventeen years—in the War of 1812. He prepared for Princeton but did not enter. He later was in partnership with Ira Dodd, and the firm constructed at the old mill site near Bay Lane the mechanical parts for the Morris Canal. They built the stone aqueduct carrying the canal over the Passaic River at Little Falls, and also the Morris and Essex Railroad from Newark to Summit. Warren S. Baldwin, another great-grandson of David, was a well-known merchant and public man in Bloomfield. He was frequently a member of the Township

BLOOMFIELD, OLD AND NEW

Committee from 1851 to 1871, and aided in securing the State School Law of 1849. The Baldwin line to David and his large family runs as follows: Joseph, Benjamin, Benjamin, David.

Daniel Dodd of Newark was the ancestor of the Dodds of Bloomfield and Doddtown, East Orange. He came from Branford about 1668. He was appointed in March, 1678, with Edward Ball, to run the northern line of the town from the Passaic to the First Mountain. The land looked fair to the young man, and he soon thereafter surveyed a tract upon Watsesson Plain, in the valley of the Second River. The Elizabeth Town Bill in Chancery states the fact of his having secured this land. In January 18, 1697, this property and much more in various localities was confirmed to him by the East Jersey proprietors. He was chosen a deputy to the Provincial Assembly in 1692. His children, Daniel, Stephen, John and Dorcas, are said to have established homes on various tracts of the Watsesson grant. It was a grandson, Daniel, who with his wife Sarah built the well-known Dodd house at the corner of the present Franklin and Race streets in Bloomfield. The inscription on the corner-stone reads as follows: "D. S. D. Noum. 10 1719." The initials stand for "Daniel (and) Sarah Dodd." The couple held possession of their homestead in Newark, on the present Orange Street, until September 16, 1735, when they sold it to Thomas Davis for one hundred pounds. Daniel died in 1767, his wife having preceded him several years. During the Revolutionary War his son Daniel occupied the Bloomfield house, and later it came into the possession of Amos Dodd, who dwelt there until after 1830, as the Oakes map in this volume will show. The descendants of

Daniel Dodd are numerous. Moses Dodd, whose homestead in 1776 was near Toney's Brook, and Deacon Isaac Dodd, one of the first deacons of the Bloomfield Presbyterian Church, who lived between the present Park Street and Park Avenue, were descendants. General John Dodd, the village surveyor, who was succeeded by Joseph K. Oakes, and who lived in a brick house at the southwest corner of the Turnpike and Washington Avenue, was another of the family. His son, Dr. Joseph S. Dodd, whose house still stands on the high terrace opposite the Glen Ridge school, at Ridgewood and Bloomfield avenues, was the father of former Vice-Chancellor Amzi Dodd, honorary chairman of the Executive Committee of the present (1912) centennial.

Stephen Davis of the Milford group was the Davis ancestor. No record appears concerning any grant to him of land in Bloomfield. There are many records showing that Thomas Davis, his son, had acquired a number of tracts in this neighborhood near the Second and Third rivers previous to 1700. A deed in the possession of the Davis family of Bloomfield, dated November 7, 1711, in the reign of Queen Anne, conveys 111 acres in the Eastern Division of New Jersey from Thomas Wall of Middletown, Monmouth County, to Thomas Davis of Newark. Which descendant of Stephen Davis was the first to make his home on Watsesson Plain we are unable to state. Caleb, the father of Deacon Joseph Davis, died in 1783, aged sixty-six years, and his wife, Ruth, in 1793. The fine stone house occupied by Joseph Davis is still standing. It is located on Franklin Street, opposite the Baptist church. There the preliminary meetings to form the Presbyterian organization were held previous to 1800. There Gen-

DANIEL DODD HOUSE (1719)

eral Joseph Bloomfield and his wife were entertained at the time of their memorable visit in 1797. According to Dr. Charles E. Knox, in his article in Shaw's "History of Essex and Hudson Counties," a Thomas Davis gave land for a school-house "near the house of Captain John Ogden" on Franklin Street, near the present Montgomery Street, sometime before 1780, and this, he stated, was afterward exchanged by Caleb and Joseph Davis for the present school property near the First church.

The Davis line in Bloomfield appears to run as follows: Stephen, the founder, died in 1691. His sons were John, Thomas and Jonathan. Thomas (2), who was born in 1660 and died January 26, 1738, acquired much land in different parts of Essex County, and one of his deeds for property further away has been mentioned. He had seven children: Thomas, Jonathan, Stephen, James, Apphia, Sarah Ball, and Mary. From Thomas (3) descended James (4), whose will in 1748 mentions Thomas (4), who died in Bloomfield in 1780, and four daughters. It is this Thomas who gave the lot for the school. From Jonathan (3), who died in 1690, descended Caleb (4), born 1717 and died in Bloomfield 1783; and Deacon Joseph (5), born 1753, died June 5, 1827. The children of Deacon Joseph were Caleb, Charles, Joseph Austin, Henrietta, Abigail, Martha and Mary. Henrietta was the last of children to occupy the old homestead, and later a grandson, Charles M., the son of Caleb (6), resided there. Joseph Austin was the well-known physician, who is still remembered by hundreds of his former patients. Another line comes from Moses Davis, sons of whom were John, Joseph and Henry.

John Ward, called the "dishturner," and more frequently "turner," was the founder ancestor of the Wards of Watsesson Plain. He came to Newark in 1666 with the Branford group. His uncle Lawrence, the first of the settlers to be mentioned as deacon, also came at that time, but died childless four years later. Elizabeth, widow of Lawrence, owned land here in 1675. John, the turner, in 1675 had confirmed to him by the East Jersey Proprietors, forty-four acres beyond Second River, bounded on the north by property owned by his aunt, Elizabeth. Upon this land, now the center of Bloomfield, the descendants of John in time settled. Who was the first to clear the woods and build a house cannot be stated. Nathaniel, the son of John, owned property here in 1697. About 1795 Washington Avenue was called "Samuel Ward's lane." When in 1806 the turnpike was built, Samuel L. Ward, born 1748, died 1814, opened through his farm what is now a part of Broad Street. It made a short cut from the center to the Green and church. The building of the turnpike and the opening of this street determined the location of the business center of the town. The characteristic names of the Wards have been John, Josiah, Nathaniel, Lawrence, Jacob, Caleb, Matthias, and Samuel, all coming from the early settlers.

Jacob Ward, who died aged 73, on September 27, 1811, kept the public house on the point opposite the old Academy, now the German Theological Seminary. In this tavern the elections were held before Bloomfield separated from Newark. The Bloomfield elections were held there subsequently. The building was removed to its present location on Franklin Street when William K. Peters built the house now on the point.

Jacob was a brother of the Samuel who opened Broad Street. Caleb, a son of Jacob, was an artist. Caleb's sons Charles V. and Jacob C. were among the first in New Jersey to engage in daguerreotyping. Jacob C. was an artist whose pictures were frequently exhibited in New York, and were widely reproduced in steel engravings to illustrate the popular annuals, or gift books, of the nineteenth century.

The Ward line from John the "turner" to Jacob and Samuel appears to be as follows: John (1) will, 1684; Josiad (2) will, 1713; Lawrence, born 1710, died April 4, 1793; and the sons named in his will, made in 1776, were Samuel, Jacob, Jonathan, Stephen and Cornelius. The father, Lawrence, and his two sons, Jacob and Stephen, made claims for damages by the British in 1776.

Thomas Morris, whose name appears among the Milford group at Newark in 1666, was the forefather of the Morris family of Bloomfield. He died at New Haven in 1673, and it is possible that the original records read "John" instead of "Thomas," and that Thomas never left Connecticut. John (2) and his wife Elizabeth, said in 1668 to have been "late of New Haven," had two sons, John and Philip. The father, John (2), died about 1675. John (3), born the year Newark was settled, was the actual founder of the family, his brother Philip having had no children. He is called "Captain" in the records and arose from "sergeant." John cleared the land and settled personally on the tract to be later called the Morris Neighborhood. He was at one time sheriff of Essex County. He lived to the ripe age of eighty-three years, and saw great developments in this region. His deed from the Proprietors of

East Jersey for this tract and others in detail has been preserved by his descendants, and is one of the exhibits at the present centennial. The document in part reads as follows:

"This indenture made the twentie fifth day January Anno Dom; one Thousand six hundred and ninetie five, and in the seaventh yeare of the reigne of William the Third over England ye King, between the Proprietors of the Province of East New Jersey of the one part, and John Morris of Newark, in the Countye of Essex, Yeoman, of the other,—First, A Plot of Land one the East side of the Third River, Beginning at a chestnutt tree markt on foure sides, by the river side, thence running east twenty chains in breadth to a Hill, thence South fouretie five chains in Lenghth as the river runs, Also a tract on the first Branch of the Second River, Beginning at a white Oake markt on four sides, thence East fifteen chaines to another markt tree, thence South South west eight chaines as the swamp runs to another markt tree thence west f—y chaines to the white oake markt as above, thence to where it began, bounded east by land unsurveyed, south by the highway, west by John Pridden, North by Thomas Davis."

This indenture bears the signatures of Governor Andrew Hamilton, whose first term, in which he was governor of both East and West Jersey, ran from 1692 to 1697, and by five members of his council—Samuel Dennis, David Mudie, James Dundas, John Bishop and Isaac Kingsland. Hamilton was also the first Postmaster-General of America, serving from 1693 to 1703.

Thus ran the old deeds, or patents, conveying to settlers lands marked out by lines from tree to tree, and following the fitful windings of the streams. Frequently the tracts thus obtained lay in the midst of unsurveyed land.

John Morris (3) testified in the land controversies about 1740 that he had occupied his lands for many years, showing that he personally settled on his plantation near Third River. His sons were Stephen (4), who was born in 1706, and died in 1781; and John, Jr., whose will is dated 1729. Ephraim (5), the son of Stephen, married Joanna Davis, and his son Stephen (6) married in 1799 Catharine Smith. Their children were Ephraim (7), Jacob, James, Joseph, Mary, Emeline Hulin and Albert. Ephraim (7), born August 27, 1800, invented the incline planes in use on the Morris Canal, and was the original partner in the Morris and Cummings Dredging Company. His son Augustus T. succeeded him. Other children were Mary Collins, John, Stephen S. and Charles. The Morris-Haskell house, on Morris Place, remodeled somewhat by Benjamin Haskell, was the home of Jacob Morris (7), the son of Stephen (6). Two doors north is the Stephen Morris (6) house, occupied by the daughters of Ephraim's (7) sister, Emeline Hulin. Ephraim (5) was "Deacon Grumbo the Miller" in Wilson's humorous poem.

The foregoing were the families, briefly sketched, which began the settling of Bloomfield. There were others who followed them; among them the Balls and the Cadmuses, but they came later. The Balls were descendants of Edward Ball, of Branford, one of the prominent men in the Newark settlement. One of his descendants was Joseph of Bloomfield. One of Joseph's sons was Isaac, buried December 25, 1825, the father of Mark Washington Ball of Newark, now aged ninety-three years. Isaac gave the first five acres of the present

Bloomfield Cemetery to the Presbyterian Society about 1796. The Cadmus line in this region begins with Thomas, born May 7, 1707, who came from Bergen (Jersey City) to Second River (Belleville), and married there Cornelia Jeralemon on June 30, 1733. His son Thomas, the "Colonel," who was the builder of the old stone house on Washington Street, married at Second River, on June 29, 1760, Pietertie Cadmus, and they probably built their new house in Bloomfield soon after marriage, or at least within the first ten years. Colonel Cadmus was born January 16, 1736, and died 1821. He was the head of the Bloomfield military company that paraded at the reception in 1797 to General Bloomfield. He is mentioned by Stephen Dodd as having taken part in the ceremonies at the laying of the water table around the old church in 1797. His children were Elizabeth, born April 9, 1761; John, born April 8, 1763; Gitty, born August 26, 1765; Cornelia, born July 17, 1767, died September 15, 1802; Abraham, born May 15, 1770; Thomas, born July 20, 1772, married November 29, 1794, died June 9, 1826; Herman, born December 7, 1774, married December 3, 1798, died March 5, 1869; Abraham, born March 24, 1777, married November 29, 1794; Peter, born March 26, 1778; Maria, born October 26, 1780; Gitty, born July 10, 1783, died March 2, 1861, mother of Thomas Taylor.

A true picture of the life lived by these forefathers of the hamlets along Watsesson Plain would be greatly appreciated if such could be portrayed. We can for the most go only by analogy. It was a settlement built mostly on one long road. This highway, though at first a wood road, as appears from the Morris deed, must have run as far as Stone House Plains long previous to 1695.

Here and there along its course stood later a log house or frame Flemish cottage, facing almost invariably south, with such barns and outhouses as the owner needed or could afford. Before 1750 these houses were not many, and even after the Revolutionary War there were only about thirty between Watsesson Hill and the Morris Neighborhood.

At first they took their grist to the older mills below Second River, or possibly to Wigwam Brook, beyond Doddtown, Orange. When the growth of population and produce warranted mills in the neighborhood, such were built. John Morris built a saw mill in 1702, and he or his son Stephen, probably soon after, erected a grist mill.

Previous to the Revolution began the era of stone houses. The local quarries yielded a very durable freestone. Some of these Flemish brownstone houses still remain as quaint and picturesque features of the town, but most of them have been allowed to decay. The Thomas Cadmus house on Washington Street is a fine specimen of the larger type. It was probably built some ten years before the Revolution. The old Morta Winne house on the Newtown road was also a good specimen, and was dated 1766 in iron numerals. The Joseph Davis house on Franklin Street was another stone edifice of that early period.

The roads of the neighborhood were few. The road to Cranetown was the present Park Avenue, and the road to Newtown and Second River was Belleville Avenue. Another road to Cranetown led westward from the Morris grist mill to Cranetown. Washington Avenue was then Samuel Ward's Lane, and ran westward till it reached the Valley Road in Orange.

It must be remembered that westward there had been made earlier settlements than those at Bloomfield, but they were not many, and the settlers who went to Orange, Cranetown and Speertown preceded the Bloomfielders by but a few years at the most.

There is a distinction to be noted between the Dutch, who came in to the northern end of the town, and the English from Newark. The Dutch had no dread of loneliness, and probably were settled on their solitary clearings earlier than the Newarkers, who were more attached to the village life. Doubtless the settling by the Newark families had been more gradual. Probably the land was very gradually cleared, the woods cut, and the buildings erected while the owners still clung to their homesteads near the Passaic. As late as 1740 they still kept up the common fence of that town, and there was still talk about Indian attacks. From time to time some family would move out and occupy their plantation beyond the Second River.

Sometime after the discovery of copper in 1719 on the Arent Schuyler property, in the present Arlington, there seems to have been an attempt to mine copper within the territory of Watsesson Plain. There is a record made on December 18, 1735, in the town records of Newark of a vote to allow mining for copper on the "common lands" of the township, and that action may have had reference to this neighborhood. Anyway there was later extensive copper mining undertaken in Chestnut Hill west of the village, and just south of the cemetery. Some years ago while quarrying out the abundant freestone found at the corner of Bloomfield

BLOOMFIELD, OLD AND NEW

and Hillside avenues, the workmen came upon a great drift of this ancient mine. Some of the discarded tools of the workmen were discovered. The vertical shaft was northward toward the cemetery, and it was thought the drift had originally run as far as Toney's brook nearby.

When and by whose enterprise these mines were so painstakingly hollowed out and shored up with great timbers, no one seems able to state. The only documentary reference to them of an early date is that of the schoolmaster, Alexander Wilson, who wrote on August 7, 1801, to his friend, Charles Orr, at Milestown that "There is a copper mine about 300 yards from my school-house which was lately wrought and many tons of ore obtained from it. It is now neglected." It is possible that these mines were opened by the New Jersey Copper Mine Association, organized about 1793 by Jacob Mark, Philip A. Schuyler and Nicholas I. Roosevelt and others.

During the eighteenth century the inhabitants of the Watsesson region were not altogether in a state of peace and quiet. In 1745 and 1746 occurred the famous Newark riots, which caused widespread excitement, not to mention voluminous reports and papers sent home by the authorities to England. Watsesson Plain was near the front in these troubles. Many of the rioters came from this locality and some were men of honored families. The rioters passed through the neighborhood on their way to Newark from Horse Neck, Cranetown, and Stone House Plain. They were a determined lot of folks, and they meant business, however vulnerable may have been their cause legally.

An examination of the documentary material touching the riots brings out the following particulars.

When the first settlers arrived at Newark they were encouraged by the Proprietors, and especially by Carteret, to purchase their lands in fair dealings from the Indians. This they did, and it has always been a matter of pride that the English settlers of Jersey knew no Indian massacres or wars.

After gradually taking up much of the land, as we have seen, on this side of the First Mountain, they, or their descendants, began to cast longing eyes toward the rich timber and meadow lands westward to the Passaic River. The broad acres called to-day "The Great Piece" and "Little Piece" meadows, lying each side of the Passaic River, and consisting of miles of hay land, were especially valuable to the settlers. Forests covered the high ground and on the lowlands nature had spread a table of rich grass to be had for the cutting, and every spring the river inundated the meadows and prepared the fertile soil for another crop. These desirable bottom lands, it was alleged, were bought from the Indians, and when the Proprietors later disposed of them to others it made those who occupied them feel like fighting. In a statement of their case a committee of so-called rioters of Essex County explicitly say that Horse Neck, together with other places under consideration, was purchased before the passing of the act of 1703, which forbids thenceforth any individual purchases of land from the "heathen" without the sanction of the crown proprietors. The date of that transaction was September 3, 1701.

Unfortunately for the settlers, their Indian deed was gone. It had been burned up in the fire that consumed on March 7, 1744, the home of Jonathan Pierson in Newark. They found some Indians, however, who duplicated the deed March 14, 1744, and this they claimed re-established their rights.

It was claimed on the part of the Proprietors that the Horse Neck claimants had dug up the only Indian within forty miles of Newark, namely one Andrew, a bad Indian who had been forbidden to remain at Cranberry, Middlesex County, and was forced to live, along with another redman named Peter, on the north side of the Cranberry Creek. Andrew, it was alleged, had been hired by the squatters to assume the roll of a big chief, and with a few others to convey the lands anew to the settlers. It also appears that Nehemiah Baldwin, probably of Orange, who had been cutting down timber in the disputed territory and sawing the same in his mill, was arrested and jailed in Newark. A band of rioters from "the back settlement," among them men of good reputation, released him from jail and were subsequently indicted. The inhabitants of Watsesson beheld with mixed feelings these movements of armed men, and some of them were among the 300 engaged in the disturbances. The riots, it should be said, were almost bloodless, and nobody in this region was badly hurt. They were demonstrations rather than attacks, for the men engaged were capable of restraint as well as firmness. Many of the Watsesson people attended the Orange church, whose pastor, Rev. Daniel Taylor, opposed the Proprietors, and wrote a tract in defense of the rioters. Among them were a number of his parishoners, and several were indicted.

Various bits of data found in many scattered records throw light upon the years intervening between the advent of the first settlers and the Revolutionary War. They help to locate roads, mill sites and homesteads, as well as to reveal the habite and occupations of the people. Our space will permit of but a few additional items concerning this period.

One of the earliest sawmills of Bloomfield was that owned in 1743 by George Harrison. It is mentioned in the Newark town records as being one of the points on a line to divide the inhabitants of the "body of Newark" from those of "Second River." The line ran "north west to Second River, thence up the same to the Saw Mill belonging to George Harrison, thence a direct line to the North East Corner of the Plantation of Stephen Morris," and so on to the mountain at Great Notch.

Harrison's mill, located near the present Harrison Street and the Morris Canal, has gone through many changes. It became a mahogany sawmill for logs received from San Domingo, and was then transformed into Van Dyck's chocolate mill. Later Hugh F. Randolph re-established mahogany sawing, and in time sold the plant to a man named Gwinn, who turned it into a paper mill and let it to William Frame of Bloomfield, and also built another mill close by. Steam power was introduced in these two paper mills. The Gwinns built a handsome residence near the mills, which was destroyed by fire. Two little children were burned to death. The boxwood path leading to the site of the Gwinn house was long a sad memorial of the former beauty of the place.

The Harrisons, Farrands and Baldwins were the chief families numerically along the old road to Watsesson before the Revolution. Moses Farrand gave land for the school in that neighborhood, probably the Franklin school of 1758.

On the Caleb Baldwin place, long occupied by the

Kimball family, there is a handsome stone well-curb. It contains the following legend:

"Caleb Harrison did the work of this stone in ye year 1760."

Local tradition says that Caleb Harrison dwelt near Soho. It is probable that this earnest stonecutter who wrought so lastingly was a relative of the Caleb of that name who used to see visions, and who, it is said, constructed a horseless carriage of some kind which failed to move, and was thenceforth known as "Caleb Harrison's Vision."

The plant long known as Black's mill, which was operated by the water of the great pond that once extended all the way to the Bloomfield Turnpike, began its existence in the early part of the eighteenth century. On January 2, 1730, Jasper Crane, of the third generation, and Joshua Miller, entered into an agreement "to erect and sett up a turning mill on a branch of the Second River, in the road that leads to Watsesson, on the land of him the said Jasper Crane, the same mill and damm to be erected and sett up and maintained at the equal charge of them." Crane was to allow "the privilege of getting what timber and stones shall be necessary."

Early in the nineteenth century Dury Bromley and Thomas Oakes of Bloomfield built on this site a gristmill for Joseph Black of Newark. Later the little stream was called Darling's Brook from James G. Darling and his brother, who succeeded Black. The last name for the plant was Brady's Mill, and to-day nothing remains of the mill or the pond.

THE "1776" PERIOD

By Joseph F. Folsom

DURING the Revolutionary War there were no battles fought on Watsesson Plain. This quiet neighborhood, being off the important military highways, escaped the greater woes of warfare. It is true there were several incursions by the enemy. These resulted in some financial losses and more or less humor, but little bloodshed. Of course there were many worries and privations.

Bloomfield came nearest to the horrors of war in 1776. Washington's troops crossed the Acquackannonck bridge on the 21st of November, and marched down the west bank of the Passaic. They were en route from Fort Lee to Trenton in the memorable retreat, and were closely followed by the British. Washington did not find time to visit personally Watsesson Plain, nor probably did many of his troops. His army stayed five days at Newark, however, and this section may have provided some forage or supplies. The British, though somewhat in a hurry to overtake the Americans, had a little more leisure for seeing the country. Detachments went visiting among the villages off the main road, and, though not very cordially welcomed, made themselves at home. However picturesque may have been the scenery of this neighborhood at the time, nothing quite equalled the sight of a string of corn-cured hams or a shoulder of beef. The Tommy Atkins of 1776 and his Hessian ally were both hungry, and with or without thanks took what they could get. They seem to have come to Bloomfield over the Newtown road, now Belleville Avenue, and perhaps also by the old road over Franklin Hill.

One of the calls made by the British foragers on the Newtown road was at the substantial stone dwelling owned by Morta Winne, located where at present the lawns of the Essex County Isolation Hospital at Soho touch the street. This fine old house was built in 1766, and great iron numerals across its front declared the fact. The numerals are preserved in the museum of the New Jersey Historical Society. The house was left unguarded and allowed to burn down on April 7, 1908, though the county authorities had proposed to preserve it for use as an office.

As we have said, the British called at the Winne house, but evidently the door did not swing back with sufficient hospitality, for one of the troopers passed around to the rear of the house and poked his bayonet through a little window over the door leading into the back of the hallway. As one of the inmates happened to be hastening up the winding stairway at the time, the bayonet narrowly missed sticking into somebody and caused considerable fright. However, they did not burn the house, and Morta Winne lived to buy after the war with Continental money a big piece of swamp lying back of the house and along the Third River, which he named the Continental Woods. The Isolation Hospital is built on a part of the swamp.

The Bergen farm in the Newtown neighborhood was also visited. Tradition says that when farmer Bergen saw the British approaching he led out his finest horse, and giving that surprised animal a vigorous kick, sent it flying toward the woods. It was his plan for saving his valuable steed. He found it later.

There dwelt in the same locality a sensible housewife named King, probably Mrs. John King, in the stone house still standing at the corner of Belleville Avenue and Willett Street, opposite the site of the Captain Kidney house. One party of hungry Britons called upon this good woman for a bite to eat, and Mrs. King, thinking thereby to put the raiders in good humor and to save her neighbors from annoyance, prepared as lavish a repast as her larder could afford. No record of the bill of fare remains, and tradition is dumb as to the final effect produced by this conciliatory banquet.

The British seem to have reached Watsesson and to have visited most every house in the village. They carted off wearing apparel, household goods, farm produce, and silverware. Stories of how the neighbors hid their silver spoons in the well, or buried them in the garden, are still told by descendants.

A tradition that has come down through the Ward family informs us that Jacob Ward, who kept the tavern at the point where Broad and Franklin streets now converge, and whose place previous to 1812 is frequently designated in the Newark "Town Records" as the voting place for the northern section of Newark, was also raided by the British. He had an unpleasant experience.

Word came to the neighborhood that the enemy was approaching, and preparations for flight were made. Ward owned property near the spot where the Essex County Penitentiary at Caldwell is now located, and he prepared to take his family and movable effects to that remote fastness. He had sent off several loads, and had the last one, which contained furniture, and was drawn by oxen, ready to start when the raiders arrived. They captured the cart, but the owner made his escape and

BLOOMFIELD, OLD AND NEW 35

hid himself for some time in the underbrush along Toney's Brook. It is also said that the delay was caused by the family returning to get a child that had been forgotten in the excitement. It is presumed that the family reached the mountain in safety, and that the father joined them later.

When the war was over, and there was some hope that the British Government might make good the damages done by their armies, a commission was appointed by the New Jersey Legislature to gather data and push the project. Jacob Ward made claims for damages sustained in 1776 to the amount of £162 6s. 6d., and when the bill is perused it may reveal that the oxen, cart and furniture carried off were charged up.

Much light has been shed upon British depredations in Bloomfield by the "First Report of the Public Record Commission of New Jersey," published in 1899 by the Legislature of New Jersey. The compilers were General William S. Stryker, Henry Haines and William Nelson. In this pamphlet are listed by towns the names of those property owners who like Jacob Ward filed claims with the commission. These claims now on file at Trenton not only indicate the routes taken by the British marauders, and thus confirm many old traditions, but they accurately inform posterity as to who suffered losses during the war, and thus help to confirm and localize many scattered traditions. The claims are generally stated to be made for damages to property plundered or taken away by "the British Army or their adherents." Much of the plundering was done by the adherents, or "cowboys," who followed the army. They got their name from rounding up and driving off the cattle of the inhabitants.

The claimants classified as inhabitants of Wardsesson, Essex County, were, with the amounts claimed, as follows: Abel Freeman, 1776, £12; Abel Ward, 1776, £17 18s. 6d.; Widow Dorcas Lindly, £13 17s. 10d.; Thomas Pierson, 1776, £300; John Davis, 1776, £60 19s.; Joseph Davis, 1776-1781, £36 4s.; widow of John Morris, £54; widow of Jabez Baldwin, £28 8s.; Stephen Ward, 1776, £39 17s.; Lawrence Ward, 1776, £15 8s.; John Garrabrant, 1776, £20 8s.; James McGinnis, 1777-1778, £4; Samuel McChesney, 1776, £7; Moses Sharp, £17 10s.; Nicholas Garrabrant, 1776, £42; John Campbell, £10 14s. 6d.; Ephraim Morris, 1781, £100 12s.; Jacob Ward, 1776, £29 10s.; Daniel Dodd, £11 19s.; Joshua Dodd, 1776, £22 3s.; David Baldwin, £12 17s.

Ephraim Morris's claim was made for damages in 1781. Evidently the raids of 1776 were confined to the lower section of the community. The British probably came up by the Newtown road, now Belleville Avenue, and worked as far south on the Newark road as the Second River. James McGinnis, who lived on the old road near that river nearly opposite the Daniel Dodd house, was apparently not visited in 1776. His claims are for damages in 1777 and 1778. Daniel Dodd's claim is undated. The absence of the date 1776 on any of the Baldwin and Morris claims seems to indicate that the pillagers did not go far above the junction of the present Belleville Avenue and Broad Street. According to the classification of these names it seems clearly shown that the whole section from old Watsesson Mill to Morris Neighborhood had become known at the time of the Revolution as Wardsesson. Usage for obvious reasons had corrupted the original Indian name

BLOOMFIELD, OLD AND NEW 37

into one that paid its respects to the numerically dominant family of the community.

James Hoyt, in his "First Church of Orange," mentions a tradition that one James Jones of Bloomfield and his family were intercepted by the Hessians just as he was about to start for the mountains with his effects on a wagon. The whole outfit was captured, and the family sent as prisoners to New York. They afterwards went to Nova Scotia, which would seem to indicate that the British gave them land there.

Hoyt speaks also of Cornelius Jones, a brother of James, as having fled at the approach of the enemy, and to have found on his return that his house was plundered, and his hogs and cattle carried off by the Hessians. This latter item is confirmed by the claim of Cornelius Jones of Orange, on record at Trenton, for £129 1s. for losses during the war.

The exploit of a company of young patriots from the vicinity of Newtown, in the eastern section of the town, is related in Barber and Howe's "Historical Collections of New Jersey." These men, Captains John Kidney and Henry Jaroleman, with Jacob Garlaw and Halmach Jaroleman, according to the story, sledded over the meadows to Bergen Heights, and captured a British officer and some refugees who with others were having a dance in a school-house. They carried them to Morristown jail. Some manuscript notes among the papers of the late Dr. Joseph A. Davis contain information additional to the above story. The name of John Winner precedes the others, making the party of adventurers five instead of four. Winner, or properly Winne, lived in the 1766 house built by his father, Morta Winne. The refugees were under the command of Thomas Ward, and when Captain Kidney peeped into the school-house window he saw a Captain McMichael, whom he captured and carried to Morristown with the rest of the prisoners. The school-house in these notes is stated to have been at Bergen Point.

Mark W. Ball of Newark has added other incidents to the story. Mr. Ball heard from the lips of Richard Kidney, a son of Captain John, that McMichael was the only prisoner taken, and that he was brought to Kidney's stone house at the corner of the present Belleville Avenue and Willett Street, and there kept guarded over night in the second story. In the morning he took breakfast with the family, and was then taken to Morristown and turned over to the military authorities. In making the capture Kidney first secured the solitary sentinel and tied him to a tree. He then placed the fence rails against the windows to prevent the refugees from discovering how small was the attacking force. Then giving orders aloud he commanded Captain McMichael to come out personally and surrender. The school-house was in Bergen village, near by the old church and graveyard, in what is now Jersey City Heights. The party no doubt went by way of Schuyler's road, now the Belleville Turnpike, and crossed the Hackensack on the ice. A picture of Kidney's house, with its two stories, appears in Hulin's "Real and Ideal Bloomfield." It was later called the Wakely house. The facts, as given by Mr. Ball, had long been lost, and they make the old Wakely house to have been one of our most historic buildings. It is to be regretted it is destroyed. The revised story is also nearer to reason, and we are inclined to think that Barber and Howe romanced when it came to the number of prisoners. It always looked like an impossibility for the Kidney party to have carried away a group of prisoners on a wood sled and get to Morristown before morning. Mr. Ball and the Davis papers agree in making the capture one prisoner, and in being altogether reasonable in the details. There are reasons for supposing that this adventure occurred in 1779. That winter is said to have been very cold, and the Hackensack requires continued cold weather near the zero mark to freeze tight enough to carry a team. That winter the Americans were encamped at Morristown.

Other traditions have reference to the visits of Washington and the American forces. It is affirmed that Washington passed through the town, probably on his way to or from Morristown, and that with a party of officers he stopped at the door of Joseph Davis's house, opposite the present Baptist church, and asked directions or other information. This house is very old. Its owner was one of the principal men of the village in those days. Deacon Davis is also mentioned among those who made claims for damages, his bill footing up £36 4s. for losses in the years 1776 and 1781.

In his article in Shaw's "History of Essex and Hudson Counties," Dr. Knox relates a similar tradition concerning the Joseph Davis house. Washington, it was said, came to the place looking for entertainment. Finding that General Henry Knox of the artillery and some sick soldiers had already been accommodated he passed on to the Farrand house beyond Franklin Hill. Dr. Knox thought that probably this incident occurred during the retreat across the State in 1776, and assumed that Washington's army had come down from Acquackanonck over two parallel roads. Even had this been the case it is not probable that Washington personally would have come by the roundabout way. He would have pushed by the direct road to Newark, where he knew accommodations awaited him. The British were too close at his heels to allow for any detours, at least for the commander-in-chief.

Another house where Washington visited, according to family traditions, was the Moses Farrand house mentioned above. Here an old table was shown for decades at which the great general is said to have taken a meal, or something of the kind. It was said that Mr. Farrand had to be guarded at one time by American soldiers, and that the Hessians were about the house at one time.

Another Farrand family tradition states that during the Revolution a soldier was killed by the discharge of his own musket while attempting to climb the fence near the Farrand house. This story is confirmed by the account, given years ago by Jasper King, of the march through Bloomfield in the winter of 1779 of General Anthony Wayne's troops. Wayne had been encamped at the present Forest Hill, in the vicinity of the Second River, and had been ordered to remove to Morristown. The soldier, it is said, climbed the fence to see if the British were coming, which seems to have been a rather foolish move anyway looked at. Jasper King's story may be found in Hines's "Woodside."

The old Thomas Cadmus homestead, still standing on Washington Avenue, west of Toney's Brook, and called to-day "Washington's headquarters," gets its reputation from a single tradition. The story is that Hermanus Cadmus, whose father Thomas owned the place, was taken on Washington's knee in cherry time, and that he was about four years old at the time. A modern critic has scouted this cherry-tree story. He has said that

THOMAS CADMUS HOUSE

BLOOMFIELD, OLD AND NEW   41

when Washington was in Bloomfield it was bleak November, and presumably only canned fruit obtainable. Nevertheless, Hermanus Cadmus, born December 7, 1774, told the late John Oakes this personal experience with Washington and Mr. Oakes told it to the writer. The critic evidently thinks only of Washington's retreat in the fall of 1776, and forgets that he must have passed through this locality a number of times.

There is reason to suppose that Washington could have been in Bloomfield when cherries were ripe in 1780. Hermanus Cadmus would have been five years old at that time. After the engagement at Springfield the British left the State. Washington soon began to move his troops toward the Hudson. He was at Whippany on June 25th, and two days later he arrived at Ramapo. On the evening of June 25th, or the next morning, he could have been at the Cadmus house and right in the midst of cherry-picking. One road from Whippany to Ramapo ran through Hanover, Livingston, Orange, Bloomfield and Passaic. Washington could have come from Orange by way of Washington Avenue and would pass by the Cadmus house, and would naturally have halted for a visit. There is no good reason, however, to doubt the several traditions concerning Washington's visits to Bloomfield, and there are many reasons for supposing them true. No doubt he passed through the neighborhood a number of times as he journeyed back and forth between the Hudson and Morristown during the war period.

During the war members of the Orange church, of which Rev. Jedidiah Chapman was the patriotic pastor, made donations of clothing and other necessities to the American army. Many of these members resided here in

Bloomfield. In March, 1778, a very large donation was sent to the army encamped near Princeton. When the army was at Morristown supplies were sometimes purchased in Bloomfield, and the farmers carted hay to the camp.

Among the veterans of the Revolution in Bloomfield was Captain John Smith, of Cranetown, a tall, soldierly man, who used to walk down to the Bloomfield Presbyterian church in the early years of the century carrying, in warm weather, his coat on his arm, and sometimes his shoes in his hand, only replacing them before approaching the church. He was a veteran of the war.

There was also Lieutenant Dodd, who fought at Monmouth, and his son is said to have been a drummer boy at the same battle. This son, Isaac Dodd, kept the old Bloomfield tavern in the early years of this century, and used to relate this anecdote of the war. He was a drummer boy with a detachment of militia stationed at Newark in 1780, at the time when the British made a raid on that place from Staten Island, and succeeded in getting their men into the heart of the town. They fired their six-pounder up Broad Street and drove the militia out, and the boy, running with the rest, threw his drum into a convenient pigsty for safety. He found it there the next day.

Another resident of Bloomfield, John Collins, was at the storming of Stony Point. He was a native of the north of Ireland. He enlisted from Pennsylvania in the Continental Army, and after the war settled at Bloomfield. He was the father of Thomas Collins.

AFTER THE REVOLUTION

By Joseph F. Folsom

AFTER the war was over the people of Wardsesson, like all other Americans, settled down to the various vocations of life. They farmed their moderate holdings of land, and in winter carried on the work of their trades. Most everybody had a trade of some kind, whether millwright, tailor or shoemaker. There were also professional men, as doctors, lawyers, and schoolmasters. The minister had not yet been located among them. Cider made from Harrison and Canfield apples was a profitable commodity.

The citizens had a share in the town and county offices. They were elected overseers of highways, poundkeepers, assessors, and freeholders. New people began to make homes in the town. An additional school was built, the one on Watsesson, or Franklin Hill, not sufficing for the growing population.

The names of householders along the main road from the Second River to the Morris Neighborhood about the year 1796 appear on an old map reproduced in "The Church on the Green," by Knox. On the east side going north were Amos Dodd, Captain John Ogden, Nehemiah S. Baldwin, Joseph Davis, David Baldwin (near the school), Ralph Tucker, Joseph Ball, Henry Osborn, Simeon Riggs, Squire Baldwin, Ichabod Baldwin, Ephraim Morris. On the west side coming south were Silas Baldwin, Jesse Baldwin, Joseph Collins's shop, Nehemiah Baldwin, Zophar Baldwin, James Wharry, Joseph Dodd, Abraham Jeroleman, Widow Lloyd, Isaac

Dodd (corner of Cranetown road), Isaac Ward, Jacob Ward, and James McGinnis.

Previous to 1796 the locality now known as Bloomfield was a community of separated hamlets. Wardsesson was the district north and south of the Second River. Doddtown lay toward Orange. Crab Orchard lay north of the present Old First Church. Newtown was toward Belleville, on the present Belleville Avenue. Morris Neighborhood was near the Third River, and still farther away was the Stone House Plains.

The immediate occasion that brought the scattered sections of the community into closer relations, and led to the choice of a comprehensive name, was the proposal, in 1794, to form a church. Most of the people were Presbyterians, affiliated either with the First Church at Newark, or the Second Church of Newark, located at Orange. It was designed to form a parish and build a church that would be more convenient for attendants living in the various sections of the community than were the older churches. When the name Bloomfield was chosen it designated not a municipality, but a parish. Bloomfield, like Orange, was simply a neighborhood of Newark. The new name occurs for the first time in the Newark Town Records under date of April 8, 1799, when certain citizens of this locality were elected overseers of highways for "Bloomfield." In 1806 Bloomfield became one of the three wards of Newark, and in 1812 the one time parish, with Belleville added, became an incorporated town.

The special meeting called to name the parish was held on October 13, 1796. The proceedings have been described in a letter written forty-two years afterward by Isaac Watts Crane, the secretary of the meeting.

BLOOMFIELD, OLD AND NEW

Writing from Bridgeton, New Jersey, February 28, 1842, the aged man said in part:

"Some time in the spring of 1797 (correctly October 13, 1796) the trustees of the Presbyterian Society at Wardsesson, being about to assume a corporate name, and desirous of having the voice of the people on the subject, caused public notice to be given of a meeting at the school-house, near the house of Isaac Dodd, Esq., of which meeting Isaac Dodd was chosen (if I recollect right) chairman, and myself secretary. Several names were proposed, viz., Jefferson, Randolph, Greenfield, and Bloomingfield, when I proposed the name of General Bloomfield. There were present those who had served under him in the Western expedition of 1794, and who bore testimony to the benevolence of his character, his kindness, and his disposition, as the soldier's friend, to promote the comfort of the troops under his command. The result was a vote, unanimous, or nearly so, in favor of the name of Bloomfield, which the trustees assumed, and a certificate thereof was transmitted to the clerk of the county to be recorded.

"I wrote General Bloomfield and informed him of this occurrence by Mr. Abraham Ogden, who was going to Trenton to attend the supreme court. In my letter I stated that the society were about building a church. In his answer he expressed his acknowledgment for the unexpected honor, and promised to make a visit to the society on the 5th of July, when he would contribute his mite to the building of the church. He was engaged on the 4th to deliver the anniversary address before the Society of the Cincinnati at Elizabeth Town. On the 5th a very large meeting assembled on the Green, and an address was delivered by General B., expressing the most kindly feelings, which was responded to by myself on behalf of the society. General B. requested me to accompany him to the library, and at his request I made out and furnished him with a catalogue, he wishing, as he said, to know what it contained, that he might present it with such as it had not.

"The amount of his donation in books and cash you must know better than I do. Mrs. B., who accompanied her husband, presented the society with an elegant gilt Bible."

The amount given by the General was $140, and he presented about 150 volumes. These books, many of them containing his bookplate, drifted about in various libraries, including that of the Eucleian Society, and were last seen in the Temperance Hall, and given to a mission on Glenwood Avenue about the time the Baptist Church bought the hall of the Women's Christian Temperance Union.

On the occasion of General Bloomfield's visit a big supply of apple butter was necessary for the feast. The only kettle large enough for the purpose was owned by Isaac Dodd. Many years afterward this brass utensil was purchased at auction by Mark W. Ball for ten dollars, and is still preserved at Newark. The new owner had the top of this historic relic cut down and refinished at Joseph B. Harvey's tin shop because it had become somewhat perforated through long use.

The course of events beginning in 1794 with the definite agitation for a local church, and terminating in 1800 with the completion of the "church on the Green," has recently been clearly and chronologically written by Amzi Dodd. It may be read in the "Register and Directory" of the First Presbyterian Church, published in 1906. Judge Dodd has carefully gone over the previously printed historical sketches, and has added considerable data obtained through his own researches. The result is the best ordered sketch yet published of the period in question. The space here allowed permits only the barest outline.

Previous to 1794 there were religious meetings held which resulted in definite proposals to form at Wardsesson a local church. The promoters of the enterprise included members of the Newark and of the Orange churches. More attended at Orange because it was nearer. Ephraim Morris on May 7, 1794, appeared before the Presbytery of New York and requested on behalf of the Wardsesson people that authority be granted for the organization of a church.

The Presbytery appointed a committee to confer with committees from the Newark, Orange and Wardsesson congregations. The conference favored a new church society, and as a result a petition signed by ninety-eight persons, "heads of families and inhabitants of Wardsesson, Crane Town, New Town and Stone House Plains, requesting to be organized as the Third Presbyterian Congregation in the Township of Newark," was presented to the Presbytery on July 23, 1794. The request, which was presented by delegates Ephraim Morris, Joseph Davis, John Dodd and Stephen Fordham, was granted.

Following this action the new society began, April 30, 1795, to engage preachers to act as temporary supplies. The services were held most frequently in the house of Joseph Davis, and at times in the Franklin school-house on Watsesson Hill. Trustees were elected October 24, 1796. On October 27, 1796, a subscription was begun to raise funds for a building. On the same date a deed was made by Joseph Davis and his wife, conveying for eight pounds "That lot of land called the church lot in Bloomfield adjoining the east side of the Green, being one hundred and twenty feet in front and rear, and extending eighty feet deep; the northeast corner of said lot being distant four chains and sixty links from the south side of the New Town road, the whole containing twenty-two hundredths of an acre."

On May 18, 1797, the corner-stone was laid. During the summer of 1799 worship was held in the then unfinished church. The Presbytery of New York voted preaching supplies for the Bloomfield church on October 3, 1799, but after that date the records of that presbytery cease to make mention of the new organization which since 1794 it had fostered. There was a reason. The Rev. Abel Jackson, a member of the Associate Presbytery of Morris County, became pastor of the new church in December, 1799, and finally carried it over to that body. It was not, however, all done in a day. Elder Simeon Baldwin was delegated on May 28, 1800, to attend the New York Presbytery and request that body to install Pastor Jackson some convenient time in the fall. There was a hitch or delay somewhere, for at a church meeting on October 25, 1800, Deacon Isaac Dodd was instructed to attend a meeting of the Morris County Presbytery, and ask that body to install their pastor. The installation occurred October 29, 1800. Ten years later, on November 8, 1810, the same Presbytery dissolved Mr. Jackson's pastorate, and then the Bloomfield church, never having been entirely at home in the "Associate" body, soon swung back into more regular Presbyterianism by uniting with the new Presby-

JOSEPH DAVIS HOUSE

BLOOMFIELD, OLD AND NEW

tery of Jersey, which had been previously a part of the New York body.

The "Associate" Presbytery was a seceding body formed at Hanover, N. J., Morris County, May 3, 1780, by ministers Jacob Green of Hanover, Joseph Grover of Parsippany, Amzi Lewis of Warwick, N. Y., and Ebenezer Bradford of Madison. It was formed professedly in the interest of ecclesiastical independence, and admitted both Presbyterian and Congregational churches. There were similar associations elsewhere. The Morris County organization was ahead of its times, but lasted upwards of forty years. One of its fruits is a fund still in existence providing help for students for the ministry. The fund is under the control of the "Society of Morris County for the Promotion of Learning and Religion."

Rev. Abel Jackson, the first pastor of the Bloomfield church, was evidently a man of strong personality and decided opinions. During the first year of his ministry a powerful revival occurred, and a large number was added to the new church. Doubtless this event was the leading force to hold back for some eight years the tide of ecclesiastical controversy which brought about his dismission in 1810, and later developed into the Jackson and the Gildersleeve factions. Alexander Wilson, who taught the school near the church, caricatured Pastor Jackson as

> "The grim man of God, with voice like a trumpet,
> His pulpit each Sunday bestampt and bethumpit."

The lonely schoolmaster also noted the after effects of the revival in the enthusiastic psalm-singing of the neighborhood, but seems to have had no sympathy with the movement. Whatever the merits of the controversy over the pastor and the two presbyteries, nothing stands against the good character of the first pastor. He was prudent, too, as well as pious, for there is extant a certificate of stock in the Newark Banking and Insurance Company made out in the name of Abel Jackson about 1805.

That all the Bloomfielders were not as grim as their worthy first pastor may be gathered from the following humorous incident that occurred probably soon after Rev. Cyrus Gildersleeve was settled in 1812. The incident turned on the possession of the old brass cannon.

Mr. Jackson, after resigning in 1810, continued to reside in the village. After two years Mr. Gildersleeve was installed, and he warmly supported the Presbyterian polity, to which meanwhile the people had again returned. But the old leaven of Jacksonism still worked, and the adherents of that party worshiped in the academy. When the time for the celebration of the Fourth approached it was arranged by each of the parties to have its own celebration. It became a matter of absorbing competition, and plans were laid to get possession of the cannon. The Gildersleeveites, or "church party," got there first, however, and captured the prize, keeping it secure against the other faction, and indulging in cheerful anticipations of firing it off loud and often in the early hours of the national day. But the Jacksonites, or the "academy party," were not subdued nor discouraged, and their silence should have boded mischief.

One doughty member of that party, Thomas Collins, stole at the dead of night to the hiding place of the old cannon, and, with grim dog-in-the-manger satisfaction, drove a rat-tail file deep and hard into its touch-hole. There it stuck, and the chances of getting it out before the next day were slim for the church party. After this exploit the chuckling scout went back to gloat over the morrow with his fellow-plotters. But the Gildersleeveites were not long in ignorance of their repulse, for the spiked cannon was discovered, and for a time consternation spread through their ranks. It looked like no salutes in the morning and the triumphant jeers of the Jacksonites. One of them, Thomas Oakes, however felt sure he could drill it out before daybreak, and so with mingled hopes they dragged the heavy piece down to the blacksmith shop at the corner of Franklin and Montgomery streets, and with might and main worked till the early morning hours on the rat-tail file. Their labors were rewarded. It was drilled out, and the "academy party" was awakened in the morning by the jubilant roaring of the lately choked cannon. It blared with emphasis that day, and silenced the crestfallen party that had attempted to put it out of commission. After that the Jackson party lost ground. Whether this defeat depressed them beyond revival, or whether the Nemesis of the old war relic oppressed them for their act of vandalism, no one can tell; but the Gildersleeveites were seen to flourish like the green bay tree, and they marched at the head of the procession and fired off the cannon any time they wanted to ever afterward.

The brass cannon of this incident still survives. It was long used in more recent times by the Bloomfield Battery Association, and not only awoke the neighbors each 4th of July, but figured in the old-time presidential campaign parades. It was originally gotten from a shop in New York by Eliphalet Hall and Major

Simeon Baldwin, who were a committee to buy a town cannon. It is a handsome French field piece, and has upon it an inscription in relief. It was used, it is said, in the colonial wars.

The iron cannon, buried muzzle downward to form a post at the corner of Liberty Street and Park Place, was brought to Bloomfield after the Civil War. It was gotten by Augustus T. Morris from the navy yard at Brooklyn. It is a ship's howitzer, and stood mounted for a number of years on a wooden base at the upper end of the Green.

One of the results of the controversy over church polity was the removal of a number of the Jacksonians in 1812 to the Caldwell Church, which still remained in the Associate Presbytery. In the records of that church a note is added to the names of the members received from Bloomfield which says: "Who came here because the church of Bloomfield voted itself Presbyterian, November 6, 1812." Stephen Fordham, one of the group to go out, was an influential man in Essex County. He was appointed at the Newark town meeting of April 12, 1802, a member of a committee to "Enquire into and ascertain the privileges of the Town under the ancient Charter." The committee brought in a report the same year, which is a very useful document, relating to questions of grants, common lands, and proprietary rights. Fordham was one of the original subscribers to the fund to build the Bloomfield church, and went about soliciting subscriptions. His home was in Cranetown, and he was buried at Caldwell. He was born in 1754, and died November 29, 1829.

Other names in the Caldwell records designated by the previously mentioned note as members who left the

Bloomfield church because of its change of polity, are Oliver Crane and wife; Stephen Fordham and wife; Zadock Crane and wife; Lewis Baldwin and wife; Fanny Crane, wife of Jonah Crane; Maria Collins, wife of Thomas Collins; and John Cockefair.

Bloomfield was thick with events at the close of the eighteenth century. With the organization of the church were grouped the naming of the town, the purchase of the Green, and the opening of the burying-ground, not to mention Alexander Wilson.

The burying-ground was given by Isaac Ball, and the first to be buried there was John Luke, who lived on the Cranetown road, now Park Avenue, near State Street. There were five acres in the original plot, and to the north was the property of Isaac Ball, where about 1810 they dug clay and made bricks for the Bloomfield Academy. The "brick pits" became in time a perpetual pond, where there were catfish to be caught, and in winter it provided the earliest skating pond. The cemetery was enlarged about 1850 through the purchase from James Ball, son of Isaac, of twenty acres. At the same time it was incorporated, with Dr. J. A. Davis, David Conger, Mark W. Ball, and William K. Peters as trustees. James Ball had been at the point of selling the land to Major Simeon Baldwin, but at the request of his brother Mark, it was secured for the church. The ground was surveyed by R. L. Cooke, son of the school matron, and cost about $1,500.

The "boss mason" who erected the Presbyterian church was Aury King. His home was east of the hill on the Newtown road, where afterward the father of Edmund H. Davey lived. The house still stands. Aury King had been a soldier in the Revolution. He lies buried in the old cemetery, and John Oakes, in September, 1902, paid him the following quaint and beautiful tribute, which as previously printed in Hulin's "Real and Ideal Bloomfield," runs as follows:

AURY KING'S MONUMENT

Wandering thro' the grounds of the dead
I came to a humble stone on which I read
These words: "To the memory of Aury King."
The stone had no eulogy or praises to sing:
Simply "Died in eighteen forty-six, aged 92."
Turning eastward from his grave on the hill I view
His monument—the walls of a church of stone,
Against which a century's storms have blown;
Yet the stones are as even, the joints are as true
As when as master-mason he laid them up new.
From the upheld spire the bell will outring:
"These walls below are a monument to Boss Aury King."

The stone used to build the church mostly was quarried opposite the copper mills at Soho. From there came particularly the three great stones at the three doors. Some of the stone came from a quarry near Toney's Brook and the Bromley property. Isaac Ball was one of the quarrymen.

The Bloomfield Green was purchased for $200 from Joseph Davis for a military training ground. The deed given by Squire Davis to the trustees, Samuel Ward, Joseph Woodruff, Nathaniel Crane and John Dodd, is dated November 27, 1797. This was five months after the visit of General Joseph Bloomfield and the exercises on the "Green," which shows that for some time the grounds had been used for public purposes by permission of its owner. The deed definitely mentions "the meeting house lot" as one of the boundaries of the

BLOOMFIELD, OLD AND NEW

Green, which proves that the church itself was not built on the parade ground, whatever of the present large area of the church lot above Beach Street may have been originally included in the public green. The lines mentioned in the deed began at the southwest corner of the school lot. There was a subscription taken up by Israel Crane and General John Dodd to secure the park, but the required amount was not raised. Joseph Davis generously gave the deed and overlooked the shortage. There is extant a copy of the deed, but the original is said to be lost. It was printed in the Bloomfield *Record*, December 4, 1873.

The "American Ornithologist" Alexander Wilson, as previously mentioned, was during 1801 the village schoolmaster of Bloomfield.

It appears that Wilson came to Bloomfield between May 1 and July 12, 1801, for, according to one of his letters, he was in Philadelphia on the former date, and his first Bloomfield letter to his friend, Charles Orr, of Philadelphia, was dated July 12th. All of his Bloomfield letters extant were written to Orr, whose address was in care of "Mr. Dobson's Bookstore, Second, between Market and Chestnut." The first reads, in part, as follows:

"If this letter reaches you, it will inform you that I keep school at 12s. per quarter, York currency, with 35 scholars, and pay 12s. per week for board, and 4s. additional for washing, and 4s. per week for my horse. I stayed only one night in York, and being completely run out, except about three 11-penny bits, I took the first school from absolute necessity that I could find. I live six miles from Newark and twelve miles from New York, in a settlement of Presbyterians. They pay their minister £250 a year for preaching twice a week, and their teacher (Wilson himself) $40 a quarter for the most spirit-sinking, laborious work, six, I may say, twelve times weekly. I have no company and live unknowing and unknown."

In a later letter Wilson thus describes the school and church in Bloomfield:

"The school-house in which I teach is situated at the extremity of a spacious level plain of sand, thinly covered with grass. In the center of this plain stands a newly erected stone meeting-house, 80 feet by 60, which forms a striking contrast with my sanctum sanctorum, which has been framed of logs some 100 years ago, and looks like an old sentry box. The scholars have been accustomed to great liberties by their former teacher. I was told that the people did not like to have their children punished, but I began with such a system of terror as soon established my authority most effectively. I succeeded in teaching them to read, and I care for none of their objections."

Wilson concluded his letter with the following story, which can be added to the witch lore of New Jersey:

"The following anecdote will give some idea of the people's character. A man was taken sick a few weeks ago and got deranged. It was universally said that he was bewitched by an old woman who lived adjoining. This was the opinion of the Dutch doctor who attended him, and at whose request a warrant was procured from the justice for bringing the witch before the sick man, who, after tearing the old woman's flesh with his nails till the blood came, sent her home and afterward recovered. This is a fact. The justice who granted the warrant went through among the people with me. I intend to visit the poor woman myself, and publish it to the world in the Newark newspapers for the amusement of New Jersey."

Possibly the Dutch doctor was the Hessian Doctor Bohn of Verona, who used, it was said, some magic in his practice.

In one of his letters Wilson told Orr that the bones of a mammoth had been discovered in Bloomfield, and in a subsequent letter, July 23d, he gave the details as follows:

"The gentlemen who discovered the bones of which I spoke is Mr. Kenzie, who was sinking a well for his paper mill in a swamp supposed formerly to have been the bed of a small creek that runs near. . . . Six feet from the surface, under a stratum of sand four inches deep, they found several bones, apparently belonging to the tail, six inches in breadth, with a part of a leg bone measuring upward of seven inches in diameter, at the joint, part of a rib four feet long, and many fragments in a decayed state."

The Mr. Kenzie mentioned in this letter was Charles Kinsey, afterward a member of Congress. He invented a machine for making paper, and he was at the time erecting a mill along Second River, near the Daniel Dodd house, and back of the present "brick row" on Franklin Street. He also erected a mill at Paterson. A fine portrait of Kinsey is in the library of the New Jersey Historical Society. Kinsey's mill was afterward operated by Eliphalet Hall and Jacob K. Meade. They made there about 1818 the paper used for "Riley's Narrative of the Wreck of the Brig Commerce," a popular book in its day. The "Coggeshall House" on Race Street was Meade's home. Next door west lived his partner. The John Oakes map shows the location. Wilson lampooned the Bloomfield folks without good reason. His letters show he had a burden on his mind when he came here. He had had some affair of the heart back in Pennsylvania, and his better feelings were held in leash. There seems to have been but one person in the village for whom he felt very much regard. That was James Gibb, an artist, or teacher, who also was a Scot, having been born in Paisley, February 5, 1775. To Gibb, in 1812, Wilson wrote a letter which is not included in the published collection. It was recently advertised for sale by an Edinburgh bookseller. If obtained it might throw more light on Wilson's associations in Bloomfield. James Gibb married Lydia, the daughter of Bethuel and Hannah Ward. Lydia Gibb died November 28, 1834. Both are buried in the Bloomfield cemetery.

Wilson's poem, "The Dominie," was written at Bloomfield, and published September 8, 1801, in the *Sentinel of Freedom*, at Newark. It runs as follows:

"THE DOMINIE"

Of all professions that this world has known,
From clowns and cobblers upwards to the throne;
From the grave architect of Greece and Rome,
Down to the framer of a farthing broom,
The worst for care and undeserved abuse,
The first in real dignity and use,
(If kind to teach and diligent to rule)
Is the learned master of a little school,
Not he who guides the legs or skills the clown
To square his fists, and knock his fellow down;

Not he who shows the still more barbarous art
To parry thrusts and pierce the unguarded heart;
But that good man who, faithful to his charge,
Still toils, the opening reason to enlarge;
And leads the growing mind through every stage,
From humble A B C to God's own page;
From black, rough pothooks, horrid to the sight,
To fairest lines that float o'er purest white;
From numeration, through an opening way,
Till dark Annuities seem clear as day;
Pours o'er the mind a flood of mental light,
Expands its wings and gives its powers for flight,
Till earth's remotest bound and heaven's bright train
He trace, weigh, measure, picture and explain.
If such his toils, sure honor and regard,
And wealth and fame shall be his dear reward;
Sure every tongue will utter forth his praise,
And blessings gild the even of his days!
Yes—blessed, indeed, by cold, ungrateful scorn,
With study pale, by daily crosses worn,
Despised by those who to his labor owe
All that they read, and almost all they know,
Condemned, each tedious day, such cares to bear
As well might drive e'en Patience to despair;
The partial parent's taunt—the idler dull—
The blockhead's dark, impenetrable skull—
The endless round of A B C's whole train,
Repeated o'er ten thousand times in vain,
Placed on a point, the object of each sneer,
His faults enlarged, his merits disappear;
If mild—"Our lazy master loves his ease,
The boys at school do anything they please."
If rigid—"He's a cross, hard-hearted wretch,
He drives the children stupid with his birch.
My child, with gentle means, will mind a breath;
But frowns and flogging frighten him to death."

Do as he will his conduct is arraigned,
And dear the little that he gets is gained;
E'en that is given him, on the quarter day,
With looks that call it—money thrown away.
Just Heaven! who knows the unremitting care
And deep solicitude that teachers share,
If such their fate, by thy divine control,
O give them help and fortitude of soul!
Souls that disdain the murderous tongue of Fame,
And strength to make the sturdiest of them tame;
Grant this, ye powers! to dominies distrest,
Their sharp-tailed hickories will do the rest.

Wilson caricatured the Bloomfield horse in the following stanza:

Here old Rosinantes their bare bones uprearing,
Move past us as if Death's horrid steed were appearing;
Dogs snuff, turkey buzzards swarm round for a picking,
And tanners look out, and prepare for a sticking.
Here's the one-handed plow, like an old crooked rafter,
The genius of farming surveys it with laughter.

Wilson did not take to the gentler sex, whom he caricatured thus: "Like ducks in their gait—like pumpkins their faces."

Wilson has at least thrown light, however discolored, upon Bloomfield and its people more than a century ago. It is easy to sift away the prejudice, and find remaining in his letters certain facts about the village worth knowing. Good Deacon Ephraim Morris, who died May 15, 1814, was lampooned as "Grumbo the Miller" whose Dutchman, Hans, operated the plant while the deacon was engaged at the church. We can plainly see through this caricature the sturdy miller, well known and active, whose vigorous influence was felt wherever he moved.

BLOOMFIELD, OLD AND NEW

The men of Bloomfield in the first half of the nineteenth century generally followed some trade. Few of them were "scribes," and the commuter had not yet come upon the scene. To accompany the valuable map which appears in this volume the compiler, John Oakes, supplied the vocations of the residents of the town about 1830. They were intelligent men, interested in education, and capable of thinking for themselves. The list, or business directory, for 1830, is as follows:

Morris family, farmers, saw mill, grist mill, blacksmith shop, owners of four-horse stages running to New York; Isaac Collins, carpenter; Samuel Pitt, storekeeper, owner of cider and also paper mill; Charles H. Osborn, carpenter; James Ball, carpenter; John Moore, papermaker at Pitt's mill; Simeon Baldwin, boss carpenter; Jonathan Dodd, cooper; Captain Benjamin Tucker, sloop between Newark and New York; Joel Dunham, millwright; Michael Chitterling, carpetweaver; Gorline Doremus, storekeeper; Isaac Ward, paper mill, made by hand; Brower, pasteboard mill; Hiram Dodd, deceased, was a millwright; Herman Cadmus, farmer; Brower, father of Samuel, pasteboard maker; Abijah Dodd, farmer; Silas Monroe, shoe shop; Dury Bromley, boss millwright, repairer, saw mill; Jotham Ward, shoe shop; Thomas Collins, stone-cutter, tombstones; Joseph Farrand Ward, farmer and carpenter; Daniel Thompson, wheelwright shop; M. D. Thomas, storekeeper at the Center; Caleb Ward, artist; Abitha Ward, shoe shop; Ira Dodd, mason, bridge builder and farmer; Abraham Cadmus, farmer; Captain Benjamin Church, sea captain; Aaron Ballard, farmer, stage driver; Rev. Cyrus Gildersleeve, retired; Joseph Collins, tailor shop; Zophar Baldwin Dodd, tailor shop;

Matthias Bowden, paper maker; Squire Joseph Davis, died 1827, farmer; Isaac Dodd, mason; Thomas Spear, watchmaker; repair shop; Isaac Dodd, tavern keeper, had been drummer in Revolution; Dr. Eleazar D. Ward, physician; Dr. Joseph S. Dodd, physician, then had office in Mrs. Henry King's house; Bethuel Ward, storekeeper; Daniel Dodd, farmer; Amos Dodd, shoe shop; Jacob K. Meade, tanner, squire, etc.; Eliphalet Hall, squire, had manufactured paper with Meade; Josiah Fairchild, hatter, hat shop; Matthias Baldwin, shoe shop; Isaac Baldwin, boss carpenter; Charles Wharry, butcher; James Wharry, carpenter; James Gibb, artist, friend of Alexander Wilson (the house later occupied by the mother of A. Oakie Hall); Smith Ward, storekeeper; Linus Ward, storekeeper; Moses Condit, farmer, man of all work; Eli Baldwin, shoe shop; Israel Ward, shoe shop; William Williamson, had been quarryman; Horton, tin peddler, traveled with a one-horse wagon, lived in house owned by Ira Dodd; Rev. Gideon N. Judd, pastor of Presbyterian Church, lived in the Captain Church house.

Zophar Baldwin Dodd, mentioned in the above directory, originated in Bloomfield the idea of planting elms. The famous trees around the Green are about eighty-five years old. In 1826 he visited New Haven and was impressed by the great elms of that town. The next year, 1827, he planted the elms now standing in front of the German Theological Seminary, and the following year those at the foot of the Green, opposite the present Church of the Sacred Heart. Following his example, other residents whose property adjoined the Green set out trees. Among these at various times were R. L. Cooke and Mark W. Ball. The trees in the center

BLOOMFIELD, OLD AND NEW 63

of the park were set out later by R. L. Cooke. There is a large elm on the old High School grounds standing alone near Broad Street whose age is also definitely known. It was planted with some others one day in the year 1830 by Thomas Collins. John Oakes watched him remove some poplar trees set out in 1809, and Thomas Collins told the boy it was now the twenty-first birthday of his son Alfred Marvin, and that the poplars planted at his birth having proved unsatisfactory, he was about to plant elms instead.

Thomas Spear, about 1830, lived in a double house on the north side of Liberty Street. In the east end of that house lived Jane Crane and her widowed mother. The first piano owned in Bloomfield was owned by Jane, and made music there. The first musical instrument used in the old church was the big base viol of Caleb Ward. After some opposition Caleb was allowed to sit in the midst of the choir in the center gallery and accompany the singers. The first band of wind instruments was brought to Bloomfield by Thomas Collins. The players came from Newark and other places, and gave a primitive band concert one summer evening at the Collins house.

The limits of this chapter have long been exceeded. The much left to be said must in this volume be left unsaid. Other chapters contain material about more recent times. The surface, however, has been merely scratched. There remains for the writer of this chapter the duty of recognizing the brave boys of 1861, who went down to the front in the War of the Rebellion, though the subject falls outside his alloted department. The following itinerary of the regiment in which the Bloomfield veterans of the Grand Army of the Republic served has been furnished by Recorder George W. Cadmus, as also the roll of the company. They are valuable historical documents. The story of the regiment is as follows:

"The 26th New Jersey Volunteer Infantry was organized on September 3, 1862; and mustered in at Newark, N. J., September 18, 1862, by Captain S. M. Sprole, 4th United States Infantry. During its term of service it had the following field officers: Andrew Morrison, Colonel; Thomas A. Colt and Edward Martindale, Lieutenant-Colonels; J. W. DeCamp and William W. Morris, Majors; Amos J. Cummings, Sergeant Major; Adjutant, John C. White; Quartermaster, John H. Bailey; Quartermaster Sergeant, Ira Kilburn; Surgeon, Luther G. Thomas; Chaplain, D. T. Morrill. Moved to Washington, D. C., September 26, 1862.

"Assigned to General Henry S. Briggs, provisional command Army of the Potomac, September 30, 1862. Served in the 2d Brigade, 2d Division, 6th Army Corps, Army of the Potomac, from October 11, 1862. General W. T. H. Brooks, Colonel Henry Whiting and Colonel L. A. Grant commanding the Brigade; Major General William F. Smith and Brigadier General A. P. Howe, the Division; and Major General John Sedgwick, the corps. Reported to General Banks, commanding the defenses of Washington, December 27, 1862.

"Moved with General Briggs, provisional command, to Frederick, Md., September 30, 1863, to join the 6th Army Corps. Attached to the 2d Brigade, 2d Division, at Hagerstown, Md., October 11th. 'This Brigade was known as the First Vermont Brigade,' composed of the 2d, 3d, 4th, 5th, 6th Vermont and 26th New Jersey Volunteers. Remained at Hagerstown until October

BLOOMFIELD, OLD AND NEW

31st. Marched to and crossed the Potomac at Berlin, Md., October 31st to November 2d. Advanced into Virginia, November 6th. Reached Upperville, November 5th; White Plains, November 6th; New Baltimore, November 9th. Marched to Stafford C. H., November 16th-17th; and to White Oak Church, December 4th-6th. Battle of Fredericksburg, Va., December 12th-15th. Crossed the Rappahannock at Franklin's Crossing or Deep Run, December 12th; deployed in line of battle, advanced and occupied positions on the Richmond Road and Deep Creek until December 15th. Winter quarters near Bell Plain Landing, December 20, 1862, to April 28, 1863.

"Mud march, January 20-23, 1863. Fatigue duty with the pontoons, January 21st-22d. Chancellorsville campaign, April 28th to May 6th. Operations at Franklin's Crossing, April 29th to May 2d. Guard of pontoon train to Bank's Ford, night of April 30th. Crossed the Rappahannock at Deep Run, evening of May 2d; and moved to position on Hazel Run, before day, May 3d. Second battle of Fredericksburg, May 3-4, 1863. Assault and capture of Mayres Heights and occupation of Fredericksburg, May 3d. Battle of Salem Church, May 3d and 4th. Actions on Dowman's Farm and near Banks' Ford, May 4th. With the Rear Guard covered the crossing of the 6th Corps at Banks' Ford. Crossed the river night of May 4th, and assisted in removing the pontoons, morning of May 5th. Returned to camp at Bell Plain, May 8th. Operations at Franklin's Crossing or Deep Run Ravine, June 5th to 10th.

"Colonel Grant, commanding the brigade, reported as follows: 'The troops were ordered forward to drive the enemy from the rifle pits on the opposite side of the Rappahannock at Franklin's Crossing; they rushed gallantly down the bank and under a galling fire launched the pontoons, rowed across, charged the rifle pits, captured them with many prisoners. It was an exciting and brilliant affair, and no account can do justice to officers and men engaged.' Occupied a position in the front line of battle across the Bowling Green Road, near the Bernard House, June 6th and 7th; with the Brigade held the front in face of the enemy for about fifty hours. Relieved from duty at the front, June 14th. Moved to Washington, D. C., June 14th-17th; thence to Newark, N. J., June 19th. Mustered out June 27, 1863. Expiration of service."

The following is a list of Company F, 26th Regiment, New Jersey Volunteers, 2d Brigade, 2d Division, 6th Army Corps. In this list those still living are so designated, the others have died. Where any have been wounded, taken prisoner or killed in battle, the fact is stated; and those not of Bloomfield have their residence suffixed.

Captains.—Walter H. Dodd; Robert J. Beach.

Lieutenants.—William R. Taylor, Montclair; Francis Danbacker, living.

Sergeants.—Ira S. Dodd, living; George W. Cadmus, living; John M. Wheeler, Montclair, killed in battle; Charles Litteel.

Corporals.—Joseph W. Nason, Montclair, killed in battle; Joseph B. Osborn, wounded in battle; William Egbertson, Montclair, wounded in battle; James H. Williams, Montclair; John M. Corby, Montclair, taken prisoners; John H. Cockefair, living; Edwin F. Dodd, Montclair, living; William H. Baldwin.

BLOOMFIELD, OLD AND NEW 67

Drummers.—Frederick Collins, living; Charles H. Garabrant.

Wagoners.—David Post; Charles Twiggs.

Privates.—John Ackerman, taken prisoner; Thomas Andrews; Peter Arnolds, Montclair; August Baldwin; Joseph Baldwin, wounded in battle; George M. Ball, living; Andrew Brady; Egbert Bush, Caldwell; James H. Cadmus; Peter H. Cadmus; Alfred T. H. Church; Ephraim Cockefair; John Collins; Henry A. Corby, Montclair; William H. Corby, Montclair; Henry M. Crane, wounded in battle; James B. Crane, Montclair, living; Joseph G. Crowell; Edwin Dodd; Horace Dodd, living; Samuel W. Dodd; Eli Drew, living; Cornelius Delhagan, Montclair, living; Daniel Delhagan, living; George W. Ellis; Hamilton W. Ellis, wounded in battle; Frederick Fairchild; Edson J. Fairchild; Edwin H. Freeman; Frederick Fitchett; Henry Glass, living; John Gattschalk; William Goud, Jr.; William Griffen; Monrow Harrison; Ambrose F. Harvey, wounded in battle; John Henieon, Caldwell, living; Lewis Herrings, living; Peter Angold, Montclair; Richard Jacobus, living; Charles Johnson, Montclair; Balthaser Kentz; Charles G. Keyler, living; William Koroger; Andrew Lampeter; Charles Leist, Montclair; Elias N. Bettell, Montclair; Charles M. Lockwood, living; John A. Magill, wounded in battle; Samuel Magill, living; Michael Maher; Theodore E. McGarry; James J. Messeler, living; Robert A. Morris; Michael Mullharion; Joseph M. Osborn, wounded in battle, living; Stephen W. Penney, Newark; John D. Penn, Montclair; George W. Post, Montclair; Joseph W. Penn, Montclair; Aaron R. Quimby, living; William Riker, Montclair; George Sidell; William Simcox, wounded in battle, living; Thomas Summervill; John W. Spear; John Speller; Henry Taylor, wounded; Samuel Howell; Charles Twiggs; George Ungamah, Montclair; John G. Vangeison; Mortimer Whitehead, Montclair.

Discharged from Service.—Newton Peaney, Newark, sick; died same day.

Died in Service.—John W. Wheeler, Montclair, killed in battle; Henry Hoffman; Charles Littell; Peter Kings, Montclair.

In order to memorialize these patriotic men, and all other Bloomfield soldiers and sailors who served in any of the wars of the past, there is being prepared a noble monument to be erected at this present (1912) centennial celebration. It will stand on the small triangular park at the corner of Broad and Franklin streets, and by its commanding position attract the eye of every passerby. Five generous contributions made possible this memorial, the amount reaching $3,000. With this encouraging start assured the required total came quickly. Bloomfield has added to its beauty by honoring the brave.

○ COPYRIGHTED ◦ DESIGNED ◦ AND ◦ EXECUTED BY ◦
○ SALLY ◦ JAMES ◦ FARNHAM ◦

Monument in Memory of the Citizens of Bloomfield who served in the Army and Navy of the United States. Erected in 1912 in connection with the Celebration of the Centennial of the Incorporation of the Town

INCORPORATION AND SUBSEQUENT GOVERNMENT

By RAYMOND F. DAVIS

PREVIOUS to the year 1812, Bloomfield, as well as many of the other municipalities of this section of the State, was a part of the Township of Newark. In 1806 Newark was divided into three wards, called Newark Ward, Orange Ward and Bloomfield Ward. Bloomfield Ward was unofficially subdivided into sections for convenience in designating particular localities. Among these we find Cranetown, Second River, Watsesson Plain, Newtown, Morris Neighborhood and Stone House Plain. Some of these names have been handed down and are still in use.

This section of New Jersey was first settled in May, 1666, by Colonists from Connecticut, and for one hundred and forty years all of the Newark territory extending from the Orange Mountains to the Passaic River remained under one government. The township of Orange was set apart by the Legislature on November 27, 1806, and then the inhabitants of the northern portion of the remaining Newark territory stirred themselves, and also decided that it would be advisable to have a separate government. As a result of this decision, on January 24, 1812, the Council and General Assembly of New Jersey passed an act setting off a new township from the Township of Newark, and incorporated it by the name of "The inhabitants of the township of Bloomfield in the County of Essex." This act, which is printed in an appendix in this volume, provided that it should not be effective until the fourth Monday of March (March 23), 1812. The act further provided that the first Town Meeting should be held at the house of Isaac Ward on the second Monday in April, 1812.

Hence, March 23, 1812, marks the beginning of Bloomfield's individual entity as an incorporated government; and on April 12, 1812, the first meeting of Bloomfield's governing body was held.

At these annual Town Meetings members of the Township Committee and other officers were elected, and various questions now decided by the Town Council were voted upon by all of the qualified voters present.

This rather indefinite form of government was satisfactory at that time, for the wants of the community were few and the times were not particularly progressive. Bloomfield Township at this time contained the territory now comprising Montclair, Glen Ridge, Franklin, Nutley and Belleville, and part of the Woodside, and Forest Hill, sections of Newark, with a total area of 20.52 square miles, as compared to the present area of 6.38 square miles.

The Townships in those days were commonly subdivided into villages.

The New Jersey State Gazetteer of 1834 says, "The villages of the Township of Bloomfield are Belleville, Bloomfield, Spring Garden and Speertown," and gives the population of Bloomfield Village as 1,600 inhabitants.

The tract known as Belleville, which had been called by that name since 1797, became a separate township in 1839, with a population of about 2,500 people, cutting Bloomfield's census in half.

BLOOMFIELD, OLD AND NEW 71

In 1846 the New Jersey Legislature passed what is known as the Township Act of 1846, which specifically states that certain townships shall be governed thereby, among them Bloomfield. Others of Essex County included therein were Springfield, Clinton, Union, Belleville, Rahway, Westfield, New Providence, Elizabeth, Orange, Caldwell, Livingston and Newark. Union County was not set off from Essex until 1857.

This statute of 1846 states that "All who are qualified by law to vote are directed and required to assemble and hold Town Meetings on the second Monday in April Annually." These meetings were held at noon, and notices were posted in four public places by the Township Clerk, by order of the Township Committee, at least eight days previous to date of the meeting.

At these meetings the following officers were elected:

Five Freeholders, resident within the Township, to be denominated the "Township Committee."
One Clerk,
One or more Assessors,
One or more Collectors,
Three or more Freeholders to hear appeals from assessments,
Two Chosen Freeholders,
Two Surveyors of the Highways,
One or more Overseers of the Poor,
One or more Constables,
As many pound keepers and overseers of the highways as necessary,
One Judge of Election.

All of the foregoing were elected for the term of one year.

In this same year (1846) another act was passed by the Legislature entitled "An Act to authorize the inhabitants of the Township of Bloomfield, in the County of Essex, to vote by ballot at their town meetings."

As a result of these two enactments the local government assumed a more definite form, and much more interest was taken in town matters by the inhabitants.

In 1868 that part of Bloomfield formerly called West Bloomfield, or Cranetown, became incorporated as the Township of Montclair, taking nearly three thousand persons from the population of Bloomfield. Whittemore's History of Montclair states that "The erection of Montclair as a separate township was occasioned by the refusal of the citizens of Bloomfield proper to consent to the bonding of the township of Bloomfield for the purpose of constructing the Montclair Railway."

In 1871 Woodside left us, and shortly afterward (1874) Franklin established her independence. Still later, in 1895, the Borough of Glen Ridge went out. All this time the practical government of the township by the Township Committee was becoming more firmly established, and we find that two or three meetings of the Township Committee were held every month.

The earliest official record of election is that of 1871, which shows the following officers elected, and appropriations decided upon:

Judge of Election.... Charles M. Davis.
Assessor .... Joseph K. Oakes.
Collector .... Joseph A. Davis, Jr.
Clerk .... J. Banks Reford.
Chosen Freeholders ... Augustus T. Morris and William Cadmus.

Surveyor of Highways. Jos. K. Oakes and Nath'l H. Dodd.
Commis. of Appeal.... Warren S. Baldwin, David Oakes and Phineas J. Ward.
Overseer of Poor...... William R. Hall.
Town Committee ..... Samuel Benson, Samuel Potter, James C. Beach, John Hall, Phineas J. Ward, John Sherman, Abram Yerance.
Justice of the Peace... Peter Groshong.
Constable .... Charles S. Squire, Charles B. Hoff, J. Mahlon Walker, Charles Farrand.
For repair of Roads.. $6,000
" Support of Poor.. 2,500
" Contingencies ... 3,500
" Schools .... 4 per Scholar.
" Cross Walks 500
Place of holding Elections for the coming year .... Presbyterian Church Lecture Room.

Since 1871 the following persons have served as town clerks: J. Banks Reford, 1872; John Fulford Folsom, 1873-1877; Stephen Morris Hulin, 1878; Edwin Westlake, 1879-1881; E. F. Farrand, 1882-1891; William L. Johnson, 1892-1909; Raymond F. Davis, 1909-.

Those who have been chairmen of the Township Committee or Town Council since 1890 are: Theodore H. Ward, 1890, 1900, 1901; Robert S. Rudd, 1891; James C. Beach, 1892-1893; William Ford Upson, 1894; G. Lee Stout, 1895-1899. Councilmen-at-large, acting as chairmen, have been: George Peterson, 1902-1903; George Fisher, 1904.

The mayors have been as follows: George Fisher, 1905-1906; William P. Sutphen, 1907-1910; William Hauser, 1911-1912.

The following others were members of the town committee or town council at various times from 1872 to 1912: Samuel J. Potter, Phineas J. Ward, Joseph A. Davis, John Sherman, Samuel Benson, Abram Yearance, Joseph F. Sanxay, Christopher T. Unangst, Willard Richards, Cornelius Van Houten, Thomas Oakes, J. Banks Reford, Thomas E. Hayes, William F. Freeman, James W. Baldwin, Wesley B. Corby, John G. Keyler, William K. Williamson, Alfred Cockefair, Samuel Carl, Lewis Cockefair, Reuben N. Dodd, Stanford Farrand, Peter S. Cadmus, Henry K. Benson, N. H. Dodd, M. A. Dailey, James Carter, William A. Baldwin, Frank S. Benson, Walter S. Freeman, George W. Cook, Charles L. Seibert, A. T. Van Gieson, Edwin A. Rayner, Seymour P. Gilbert, Charles H. Halfpenny, Martin Hummel, A. J. Lockwood, Charles W. Powers, Benjamin Haskell, John Lawrence, Frank Foster, Thomas H. Albinson, James H. Moore, Richard K. Schuyler, James M. Walker, George M. Wood, James J. Thompson, John R. Conlan, Wilber M. Brokaw, Herbert C. Farrand, W. F. Harrison, William Douglas Moore, Charles W. Chabot, Charles J. Murray, Jesse C. Green, William B. Hepburn, Frederic M. Davis, August Fredericks, Jr., George Hummel, James C. Brown, Lewis B. Harrison, Frederick Sadler, Henry Albinson, Frank N. Unangst.

In 1883, owing to the many fires in and around Bloomfield Center, it was deemed necessary to have some regular fire protection, and in that year Essex Hook and Ladder Company No. 1 was organized. The fire

BLOOMFIELD, OLD AND NEW

truck arrived in Bloomfield on August 10, 1883, and an all day celebration took place, including a street parade and baseball games.

The following year (1884) Phœnix Hose Company No. 1 was organized, and early in 1885 Active Hose Company No. 2 was established. At a meeting, held June 10, 1885, the Township Committee officially recognized these fire companies, accepted their services, and assumed jurisdiction over the Bloomfield Fire Department and members thereof.

In 1884 a system of water pipes was laid throughout the more densely populated sections of the township, and connected with the Orange Water Works. Water was sold to the inhabitants by the Orange Water Company.

Gas pipes were laid in the principal streets in 1873 by the Montclair Gas and Water Company, and this method of lighting the town continued until 1896, when a fifteen year franchise was granted to the Suburban Electric Light and Power Company for furnishing electric light.

The sewer system was installed in 1893, at which time a contract was signed with Orange providing for the joint use of a Union Outlet Sewer. This agreement is still in force, and furnishes one of the complications in Bloomfield's consideration of the Passaic Valley Sewer project. The laying of the original sewer system necessitated a $50,000 bond issue, and extensions have been made from time to time as occasion demands. Altogether bonds have been issued to the amount of $100,000 for sewer purposes, many of which have been retired.

On the 23d day of February, 1900, the New Jersey

Legislature passed an act incorporating the Town of Bloomfield which changed the form of government from a township to a town. Accordingly the then Township Committee reorganized as the Town Council on February 26, 1900, and since that date Bloomfield has been governed by the provisions of the Town Act of 1895, which is entitled "An Act providing for the formation, establishment and government of towns," adopted March 7, 1895.

After much debate by the inhabitants of the town, the water system, including all pipes, mains, fixtures, etc., was purchased in 1904 from the Orange Water Company at a cost of $90,000. The price originally asked was $150,000, but the Council succeeded in driving a more advantageous bargain.

The Montclair Water Company, a subsidiary of the East Jersey Water Company, now supplies the town with water under a contract which expires May 1, 1925.

The contract for lighting the streets of the town expired in 1911, and in November of that year a new agreement was entered into with the Public Service Lighting Company providing for arc lamps and incandescent lights to be supplied in such streets and locations as the Council may from time to time designate. This contract is effective until March 1, 1917.

The governing body of the town has each year found problems more difficult to dispose of, and more numerous than those of former years. Such problems are, however, treated of in other pages.

The elections as conducted at the present time are not the social gatherings that were those of sixty, or even thirty, years ago, and it is safe to predict that the next hundred years will see even greater changes.

The officials of Bloomfield for the present year (1912) are as follows: Mayor, William Hauser; Clerk, Raymond F. Davis; Councilmen, Charles J. Murray, Lewis B. Harrison, George Hummel, Frederick Sadler, Henry Albinson, Frank N. Unangst; Collector, Frank Foster; Treasurer, Harry L. Osborne; Attorney, Charles F. Kocher; Overseer of Poor, Adam Lind; Physician, John D. Moore, M.D.; Superintendent Public Works, Fred B. Stimis; Superintendent Water Department, William R. Rawson; Superintendent Fire Alarm Telegraph, A. F. Olsen; Engineer, Ernest Baechlin; Chief Fire Department, Bernard F. Higgins; Chief of Police, Lewis M. Collins; Recorder, George W. Cadmus; Building Inspector, George M. Cadmus; Board of Assessors, George B. Milliken, Chairman, William R. Raab, Clerk, Robert D. Rawson; Board of Health, James J. Thompson, President, Jacob S. Wolfe, M.D., Seymour P. Gilbert, William A. Ritscher, Jr., Joseph T. Charles, Joseph C. Saile, M.D., Secretary, Registrar of Vital Statistics, and Health Inspector.

THE SCHOOLS AND SCHOOLMASTERS

By William A. Baldwin

The families of the early settlers from Branford and Milford, who in 1666 formed the Newark Colony upon the banks of the Passaic River, brought with them not only a deep religious feeling, but also a strong desire for the education of their children.

In 1676 the town meeting of Newark authorized the townmen to find a competent number of scholars and accommodations for a schoolmaster. Again, in 1693 and 1695, two acts for establishing schoolmasters were passed. Under these acts schoolmasters were employed, but there is no mention of a school-house until 1714, when it was voted at a town meeting that "ye old floor of ye meeting-house should be made use of for ye making a floor in ye School house in the middle of ye Town." This school-house was probably built soon after the passage of the above acts for establishing schools. So much of the history of the Newark Colony is given because Bloomfield was at that time an outlying section of the Town of Newark, and subject to the same government. The outlying settlements soon after 1700 no doubt developed some form of instruction independent of the incipient schools of Newark village.

The first authentic record of a school-house in Bloomfield is on the foundation stone of the Watsessing Hill school-house which announces that the original building was erected in 1758, and its addition on the east side in 1782. Both parts were built of stone. It remained standing till 1852, when it made place for the house of Jay L. Adams. Its location was near the corner of Franklin Street and Willard Avenue. Like all schools of the time it must have been small, perhaps 15 feet by 25 feet in size, poorly heated, and furnished with low benches and cheap desks; nor was it free to all, but only to those who could afford to pay the small tuition fee required.

Before its destruction the Baptist congregation, then forming, used this school building for a temporary meeting place. The corner-stone, long preserved by the late Joseph B. Maxfield, with its dates 1758 for the original structure and 1782 for the extension, is now preserved in the interior foundation wall of the new (1911) Baptist Church. The inscription on the stone is like this: "The West End of This House Built in 1758, The East End in the Year 1782."

The school bell, which hung on the top and near the rear end of this building, is now in the old high school, having been presented by the late William Cadmus. It is not improbable, in fact it is a persistent tradition, that, like the Liberty Bell in Philadelphia, it rang out its peal for liberty when the news was brought that the Declaration of Independence had been signed. A different account, stating that the bell was later used to announce the approach of trains at the old Newark and Bloomfield, now the Delaware, Lackawanna and Western Railroad depot, and afterward found an honored place in the belfry of the Episcopal Church, is erroneous. The bell used at the railroad and in the Episcopal Church was gotten by a Mr. Smith from the burned tug *Isaac Newton*.

At some time long before 1780, Thomas Davis gave

a quarter acre of land for a school-house site "near the home of Captain John Ogden," near the present corner of Franklin and Montgomery streets. But in 1782 Caleb and Joseph Davis exchanged for the quarter acre a new half-acre lot at the corner of the Newtown Road. On this new site was placed, at about 1782, a log school-house, which was there in 1801, when Alexander Wilson taught school, but was later burned and a small stone structure took its place. It may be seen back of the church in the engraving in the article on Bloomfield in Barber and Howe's "New Jersey Historical Collections," 1844, and also as reproduced in this book. After sixty-seven years the half-acre lot was enlarged by additional purchases on the east side. The little stone school-house gave way in 1849 to a substantial brick building located on the recently acquired addition, and the school-house site of 1782 became a portion of the present school playground behind the Presbyterian Church.

The Union School was situated at the corner of Morris Place and Franklin Avenue in the Morris neighborhood. A deed, given in 1845 by Stephen Morris to James Morris, Albert Morris, James Ball, Charles Osborn and Warren S. Baldwin, describes this property as already having the Union School-house upon it. Joshua C. Brokaw was the last teacher employed at this school previous to the enactment in 1849 of the free-school law, when it was merged with the Central School. Later Mrs. Isaac H. Day and Mrs. Pearson taught there a few scholars, using the building as a private school and charging a small fee. Town elections were afterward held there, and also religious services and occasional

BLOOMFIELD, OLD AND NEW

public gatherings of a political or social nature. The building was finally torn down.

The only pupil of whom we have definite knowledge as connected with the Bloomfield schools before 1790 was the boy, Stephen Dodd, then eleven years of age, who went to school at Watsessing Hill, or, as it was then probably called, the Franklin School-house. One of his teachers was, no doubt, Isaac Sergeant, whose name as schoolmaster at Wardsesson appears as a subscriber for twelve copies of "Newton on the Prophecies," published in 1787, at Elizabeth Town. Probably he re-sold the books in the neighborhood. Alexander Wilson, the celebrated ornithologist, was for about six months in 1801 the teacher in the upper school-house near the Presbyterian Church. Amzi Armstrong, a young man seventeen years of age, taught on Watsessing Hill in 1788 or 1789. He came from Florida, New York, and twenty years later, as Dr. Amzi Armstrong, became the successful principal of the academy. He studied theology under the Rev. Jedediah Chapman of Orange, while he was teaching in the Franklin School-house, and was called to be pastor of the Mendham Presbyterian Church in 1796. One of his successors was the son of Mr. Armstrong's former pastor at Florida, Amzi Lewis, Jr., who was teaching here in 1810; with him was associated Amos Holbrook. These taught in the two school-houses, alternating a month or so at a time. Other teachers in the Stone School by the church were M. D. Thomas, from Connecticut, who married a daughter of Mrs. Jane Dodd; Philander Seymour, who married Eliza Cadmus; D. Lathrop, and James Shields, who later became United States Senator from Illinois.

Soon after the beginning of the nineteenth century and long before the public school system came into operation, there opened in Bloomfield what is now known as the academy period. A number of these educational institutions, and they were of the best character, were maintained in the village.

The Academy (now the German Theological Seminary) was projected in 1807, and sufficiently furnished in 1810 for the reception of students. It was an unusual enterprise among the academies of the day. Its object was the education of young men for the ministry, and it was closely identified with the interests of the Old First Church. It seems in its day quite to have surpassed in reputation the academies of Newark and Orange, whose organizations preceded it. It absorbed the attention of the town, and as all schools then were conducted on the plan of the payment of a tuition fee, the Academy at first and afterward the Academy and Madame Cooke's school for girls quite overshadowed the common pay schools. It was built by "a society for the promotion of literature," and "for the purpose of building an academy," upon joint stock subscriptions in shares of twenty-five dollars each. Its massive brick walls have since been adorned with a mansard roof, and its color made more pleasing to the eye. Amzi Lewis, Jr., became the first principal, and was followed by Rev. Humphrey Mount Perine and Rev. John Ford. The students of the classical department were from thirty to forty in number, young men of mature age who assisted in conducting the morning devotions. The primary department in the front basement numbered at that time about seventy-five pupils. Its graduates included many who afterward became ministers, doctors of medicine, lawyers, and teachers. The Academy as thus conducted had a successful course of twenty-two years, when, because of two attacks of smallpox among the students, and certain other complications, it was closed. It was afterward conducted as a private school until 1866, the latter part of the time under the management of James H. Rundall as principal. From him it was purchased by the Board of Directors of the German Theological School. It is now occupied as a seminary for students of various nationalities, with academic and theological departments.

During the latter part of the academic period the Bloomfield Female Seminary was organized. A building facing the Common, near where the residence of Hon. Amzi Dodd now stands, was erected in 1836 for $6,000 by an association of gentlemen. Madame Cooke's School, as it was familiarly called, was expected to do for the young ladies of the town what the Academy had been doing for the young men. Mrs. Harriet Cooke had taught in Vermont, and in Augusta, Georgia. For eighteen years her seminary in Bloomfield was the center of a powerful intellectual and religious influence. Being a woman of strong and penetrating mind, and possessing great decision of character, together with quick insight, profound sympathy and deep piety, Mrs. Cooke had a strong influence over teachers, scholars and families. The celebrity of her school became established. Her rooms were filled with incomers, and her day desks with the girls and young ladies of the vicinity.

In Mrs. Cooke's "Memories of My Lifework," written by her late in life, she states that 1850 pupils had attended her school, sixteen of the teachers and students had become foreign missionaries, and many others had become teachers and home missionaries. During the period extending from 1847 to 1861, Rev. Ebenezer Seymour conducted a boarding and day school for boys and girls upon Beach Street, at the corner of Spruce, the location of which was later changed to a building on Belleville Avenue. This building was afterwards used for the Erie Railroad depot, and stood just west of the railroad.

A school for boys, under the management of Charles M. Davis, was situated on Liberty Street, corner of Spruce Street, from 1851 to 1868. Here many of the sons of wealthy New York families, sons of missionaries, as well as young men from the town, received their education. The growing efficiency of the public schools making it difficult to conduct a private school with profit, caused the closing of this school as well as other private schools which had flourished up to this time in Bloomfield.

The beginning of the free school system which we shall now consider is distinctly marked by the enactment of a special school law for the Township of Bloomfield. This law was enacted in 1849, and with it began a period of concentration and more thorough graduation. There had previously been four school districts in the township: The Central, the Union, the Franklin, and the Stone House Plains district. The Central and Union were now united in a strong organization, later known as the Central Union school district number seven. The Franklin district was absorbed.

The Stone House Plains district, comprising all that part of the township about five hundred feet north of

BLOOMFIELD FEMALE SEMINARY.
MADAME COOKE'S SCHOOL (1856)

Bay Avenue, conducted its own school. It was known as school district number six.

The first school known to exist in Brookdale, then called Stone House Plains, was erected during the last quarter of the eighteenth century. It was a frame structure and stood on the lot opposite the present home of Alexander Parsons. The furnishings of this building were of the crudest sort, such as were to be found in all of the schools of that day. They consisted of pine desks, ranged on the sides of the room and running the entire length, with benches made of rough boards, with holes bored in them at each end for the insertion of the legs. Other benches, with backboards, were provided for the use of the smaller children. These had no desks attached to them, and were placed in the middle of the room. A big Franklin stove for burning wood was used for heating. The school at that time was open only three or four months of the year, and was a pay school. The ground had been given by Peter Garrabrant, who owned considerable property in this section. The first teacher in this school was a Mr. Schermerhorn. Starr Parsons also taught for some time, being followed by Silas Merchant—who taught until the building was burned in 1835, when he moved to the Center School, near where the old High School building now stands. As the location of the Stone House Plains school was not central, another plot was acquired where the old Brookdale school building is now situated. This was also a frame structure and was plainly furnished. It was continued as a pay school until about 1849, J. William E. Davidson being the last instructor.

Moses W. Wisewell was one of the first to have charge of Brookdale after it became a free school.

Mrs. Margaret B. Jones, mother of Theodore Jones of Upper Broad Street, then known as Margaret Anna Burgess, also taught in this school about this time. Among those who served as trustees were Simeon Brown, Sylvanus Cockefair, Tunis Garrabrant, James G. Van Winkle, and Charles E. Davidson. About 1857 the frame structure was torn down, and one of brick erected at a cost of eleven hundred dollars. In 1885 an addition was made which doubled the capacity of the school. The whole building was better equipped, and a more satisfactory heating plant was installed. When the district in 1901 was merged in the town by an act of the Legislature, further improvements were made. It continued in use as a school until the new building was completed in 1910. It is now being used temporarily as a hose-house for the Brookdale Fire Department.

Coming back to the Central-Union district we find that after the enactment of the State School Law of 1849 the two school-houses in this district, the Franklin and the Central, were respectively sold and removed, the Central's lot in the rear of the Presbyterian Church doubled in size, the enlarged space appropriated for a playground, an adjoining lot on Belleville Avenue secured for a new school site, and a building erected at once.

"During this year (1849)," writes one who was then trustee, "the authorities set to work earnestly to build a school-house. The dimensions of this building were to be 32 by 64 feet. It was to be two stories high and built of brick, at a cost of twenty-five hundred dollars, which in those days appeared to many a great waste of money. They had never seen a common school with more than thirty or forty scholars, and why should so

BLOOMFIELD, OLD AND NEW   87

many seats be provided to be left empty? But one year was enough to convince the most incredulous that the building was none too large, for soon additions had to be made." The vote, as appears by the record, to build this building at the large cost of $2,500, was a very creditable one, standing thirty-six in favor to seven against. It is interesting to notice that the year before the free school law was obtained, the whole number of scholars in attendance was thirty-five at a cost of tuition for each scholar of two dollars per quarter; while the number in attendance the year after the free school law went into operation was one hundred and ninety-six, at a cost to the district of one dollar and thirty cents per quarter for each scholar.

The new Central Building was afterward enlarged, and stood for twenty-one years, until rebuilt in 1871. According to records left by Lewis B. Hardcastle, these schools were divided into a "Male Department," "Female Department," and the "Primary Department." The latter two were on the first floor, the former on the second floor. Mr. Hardcastle was the first principal of the male department, with James Stevens as assistant. There is also a record that in August, 1850, George A. Oakes, then fifteen years old, was dismissed from school to enter upon the duties of an assistant teacher. This department had an attendance of one hundred and fifteen boys from six to fifteen years of age.

Miss Dean was principal of the Female Department, for a few months assisted by Miss Virginia McCracken. On November 4, 1850, Miss Ann E. Sturdivant took charge. Although but nineteen years of age, she is remembered as a bright and competent teacher, who did much for the school, training the pupils especially in reading, declamation, singing and mathematics. This school numbered eighty-seven girls, their ages ranging from six to fifteen years.

Miss Lydia Neal was the first principal of the primary department. She was assisted by Miss Caroline Morris, daughter of James Morris, and later wife of Uzal T. Hayes. Miss Caroline Ball, afterward Mrs. Walter Freeman, also taught in this school. Other teachers were Miss Caroline Sanford, and Miss Mary Hulin, now Mrs. James M. Walker. During the first year the pupils of five to nine years of age numbered one hundred and forty-one, the various departments totaling three hundred and forty-three. The average attendance was about two hundred.

At the time this free school was established, as indicated above, there were four large boarding schools in Bloomfield. The boys and girls of the village had been accustomed to attend these "select" schools as day pupils, paying a small sum each quarter for tuition; therefore they spoke disparagingly of the new public school as a "free" school. Previous to this time also the common schools of this town, as elsewhere throughout the State except in the large cities, were pay schools; each scholar paying two dollars per quarter tuition, the school being principally supported by this fee. Schoolhouses were entirely built, and largely kept in repair, by private or individual subscriptions. The laws of the State permitted the raising of a tax on the property of the district for fuel and incidental expenses, the amount not to exceed double the amount raised each year for the support of the poor of the town. If in any township, therefore, the inhabitants were not liberal enough to subscribe a sufficient amount to build a school-house, the only alternative was to do without one, and such was the sad condition of many towns in our State.

Because of the sentiment against the new free schools, public exercises were held October, 1850, in the "Old Church on the Green" to exhibit the work of this local school. The large audience was entertained by singing and recitations, and by motion songs by the primary children. The pupils also sang for the first time publicly "The Star Spangled Banner."

Dr. Joseph Austin Davis was the first Town Superintendent of Schools. The first trustees were David Oakes, Warren S. Baldwin, Albert M. Matthews, Jr., and John L. Cooke, son of Madame Cooke. The following superintendents and principals have been employed:

Dr. Joseph Austin Davis...................1850
Lewis B. Hardcastle...................1850-1852
Warren Holden 1852
E. H. Hallock........................1852-1854
Mr. Pennington 1854
Mr. Ward 1855
Henry Austin Ventres.................1855-1865
John R. McDevitt....................1865-1868
John W. West........................1868-1870
Frank H. Morrell....................1870-1871
J. Henry Root.......................1871-1880
Benjamin Mason 1880-1881
John R. Dunbar......................1881-1897
William E. Chancellor...............1897-1904
George Morris 1904

Of the principals, Mr. Morrell is now Supervising

Principal in Irvington. Mr. Root, formerly principal of Greenwich Academy in Connecticut, is residing in Bloomfield. Mr. Dunbar, after teaching in one of the Brooklyn high schools for a number of years, is also living here. Superintendent Chancellor, who came to Bloomfield from a position as head of the history department in Erasmus Hall High School, Brooklyn, has since filled the position of Superintendent of Schools in Paterson, N. J., and Washington, D. C. He is now filling a similar position in South Norwalk, Conn.

Five of the former teachers of the High School have reached positions of considerable prominence in educational work. Everett S. Stackpole became President of the American Theological Seminary in Florence, Italy; John F. Woodhull, Professor in the Teachers College in New York City; Herbert C. Hamilton, Professor of English in Amherst College; Clarence F. Perkins, Professor of History, University of Missouri; and George C. Clancy, Professor of English in the University of Syracuse.

The longest term of service of any teacher has been that of Miss Samantha Wheeler, who was retired in 1900 on a pension from the State Teachers' Retirement Fund, after forty-two years of service. Since that time the following teachers have been retired on pensions after long years of service, viz.: Mrs. Mary L. Ellenwood, Miss Kate F. Hubbard, Miss Edith E. Hulin, Miss Anna Baird, Miss Jennie Baird and Miss Mary M. Draper. Many teachers are still in service whose names are enrolled in the grateful memory of their pupils.

Among the trustees have been David Oakes, Warren S. Baldwin (who served twenty-three years), Artemus N. Baldwin, James Morris, Robert L. Cook, Dr. Joseph

A. Davis, Eliphalet Hall, Abraham H. Cadmus, Chabrier Peloubet (who served thirty-three years), Albert Matthews, Samuel Carl, Daniel H. Temple, E. W. Page, Edmund Smith, Dr. William H. White, John Sherman (who served fifteen years), Joseph Hague, J. W. Snedeker, Rev. Dr. A. C. Frissell, A. T. Morris, V. G. Thomas, M. W. Dodd, W. J. Williamson, C. W. Maxfield, Andrew Ellor, S. Morris Hulin, F. C. Bliss, Henry Russell, Thomas Oakes (who has served thirty-two years and is still in office), William A. Baldwin (elected in 1880 and still on the Board), Frederick H. Pilch, A. H. Edgerley, Samuel Peloubet, J. Banks Reford, Edward G. Ward, Charles L. Seibert, Frederick R. Pilch, George W. Pancoast, A. J. Lockwood, Dr. John E. Wilson, Dr. J. S. Wolfe, Charles F. Kocher, Dr. William R. Broughton, Frank B. Stone, G. E. Bedell, C. H. Madole, Samuel Ellor, and Joseph F. Vogelius. The present Board of Education is organized with the following members and committees:

President—Thomas Oakes.
Vice-President—Frederic M. Davis.
Committee on Finance and Supplies—Clarence Van Winkle, William A. Baldwin, Secretary of Board.
Committee on Instruction—Frederick R. Pilch, Morgan D. Hughes, Frederic M. Davis.
Committee on Buildings—Charles Martin, James C. Brown, Arthur A. Ellor.

In some historical notes former Superintendent William E. Chancellor makes the following statement: "In the history of the schools the most prominent men have been Charles M. Davis, for twenty-five years County Superintendent and afterward Superintendent of Schools in Bayonne, who always stood for progress in

Bloomfield, where five generations of his family were born; Chabrier and Samuel Peloubet, David and Thomas Oakes, Warren S. and William A. Baldwin, and Frederick H. and Frederick R. Pilch. During the 'panic' years, after 1873, John Sherman, then Treasurer, did great service to the schools by securing large loans for the payment of the teachers' salaries in cash, rather than in warrants, a course which nearly all schools then adopted."

Following the organization of the schools previously described, the appropriations made by the district were small and sometimes grudgingly given, while little or no aid was received from the State. The furniture in use was of a primitive character, consisting of old-fashioned benches and desks, classes were not graded, and teachers were without special training. Whips and other instruments of punishment were freely used.

In the northeast corner of the Central School building, on the upper floor, was a room where, after school, boys were sent for punishment; and where the birch was freely applied to hands and knees by the principal. On one occasion a large boy seated near the door was struck by the principal, at which, gathering up his books, he took his slate and sent it skimming across the building in the direction of the teacher. It stuck in the wall, while he passed out of the school never to return. Scenes like this were not of frequent occurrence. This incident is told to show the evil passions aroused by corporal punishment, which has now been wisely prohibited by law.

Music was not a regular branch of instruction, but was taught by the teachers, as they were able, with some voluntary help from outsiders. Among those who gave occasional instructions of this kind was the popular composer of Sunday-school music, William B. Bradbury. His genial manner and earnestness aroused the scholars to unusual effort, and he was voted a great success as a leader. He was also very popular because of his uniform kindness to the pupils. On one occasion he purchased and distributed to the scholars on the green in front of the school-house large pieces of watermelon, which treat, of course, they greatly enjoyed.

During the latter portion of this early period (1850 to 1872), the modern graded system of instruction was developed which culminated in 1872 in a High School. This was preceded in 1871 by the erection of the present High School building, at a cost of thirty thousand dollars.

The first published report of the Board of Education was printed in 1872. It contained a full account of the new building, which was considered well designed and up-to-date. The ventilating system was thought to be perfect, but it subsequently proved to be worthless.

In 1872 the first steps toward establishing a high school were taken. The plan as adopted and set forth in the printed report of 1872 was as follows:

"First. The High School is established to provide those scholars who have completed the studies of the Grammar School with an opportunity of pursuing more advanced studies, and obtaining a higher English and Classical education.

"Second. The teacher must be a graduate of some respectable college.

"Third. Candidates for admission to the High School must make application during the week preceding the close of the summer vacation. Candidates must be of good moral character, they must pass a satisfactory examination in spelling, reading, writing, arithmetic, English grammar, geography, and history of the United States."

These requirements were reasonable, and if always insisted upon, would prevent criticism of the public schools for neglect of the fundamentals. We believe, however, that the policy so early laid down has been, in the Bloomfield High School, faithfully followed ever since. The first class in the High School began on January 3, 1873, with twenty-two members. At the close of the school year the trustees reported that the establishment of the high school class has already exerted a healthful influence upon the grammar schools, as shown in the increased diligence of the pupils and in the care they had taken in the monthly examinations, and in a more uniform attendance. They also added that the high school department will undoubtedly raise the standard of education to so great a degree that enough pupils will be found in each graduating class to supply the want of new teachers as the exigencies of the district may require. In this last statement we see that the teaching force was far inferior to that now secured, when none but graduates of normal schools and colleges with one or more years of experience, are placed in charge of classes. Out of the twenty-two scholars who started in 1872, eleven graduated in 1876. A few each year continued to graduate until 1879, when the Greenback party was successful at the polls, and the trustees then elected reduced both the number and the salaries of the teachers, and changed the course of study in the schools very materially. The next year new trustees were elected for a term of three years under a new law, and the schools again moved forward along progressive lines. For three years no pupils were graduated from the High School; but later, under the efficient guidance of John B. Dunbar as principal, and a board of trustees having the confidence of the community, and reasonbly secure in their offices, the High School took a strong position from which it has never since been driven. The average attendance of the Bloomfield schools at that time was four hundred, about twice what it was in 1850-1855. The net enrollment was five hundred and seventy-two. Boys and girls recited together. This was an innovation, for in former years the sexes had been entirely separated. The school library was begun in 1874 by Mr. Stackpole, then a teacher under Principal Root. The first course of study to be printed was published in the same year. In 1876 boundaries were first established between the schools, and an exhibit was sent to the Centennial Exhibition in Philadelphia. In this same year systematic examinations, designed to enforce upon teachers and scholars the exact requirements of the course of study, were first introduced.

In 1878 the parochial school of the parish of the Sacred Heart was opened. This relieved temporarily the greatly overcrowded condition of the schools.

In 1883 the Center Primary School on Liberty Street was built at a cost of ten thousand dollars.

In 1888 departments of penmanship and drawing were introduced, and the course of music, which had been taught in the school for many years, was improved. The nature study course was also greatly improved in this year, and a very successful fair was held netting eight hundred dollars, for the purchase of various apparatus for use in the schools. At this period there was carried on much industrial work in the nature of manual training.

In 1891 the High School course was revised for a three-years' course of instruction, and the subjects were made partly elective.

In 1892 the Berkeley School was re-built at a cost of about twenty thousand dollars, replacing the original Berkeley primary school, built in 1868. Again, in 1909, an addition of eight class-rooms made it the largest school building in the town. In 1893 four rooms were also added to the Center School.

In 1896 Board of Health rules relating to contagious diseases were first applied, to the marked benefit of the schools; and in the same year the present four years' course in the High School was established by taking a grade out of the grammar school, and adding it with certain changes to the High School. Following these changes kindergartens were added, the English course was extended, and the departmental system introduced in the grammar classes. Laboratories were also placed in the High School for science instruction. Manual training was introduced for all classes, embracing departments of drawing, raffia and basket work, cooking, wood-working, and metal-working. Evening schools were started providing instruction in the English branches, also typewriting, stenography and mechanical drawing. In recent years classes in English for adults of foreign birth who wish to learn the language of their adopted country have been added, also classes in wood-working, cooking and electricity for such students.

Neighborhood clubs were organized to promote the

harmonious working of the schools by bringing teachers and parents into closer touch, and increasing neighborhood pride in the schools. Free lecture courses are given each winter, which furnish much instruction and entertainment. A summer school is carried on in one neighborhood largely populated by foreigners, where the pupils devote a few hours each day to manual training and the common English branches, the work in English being very helpful to them when the studies of the regular school year are taken up.

An event of importance in the history of the schools was the formation in 1895 of the Borough of Glen Ridge out of Bloomfield Township, which took away several hundred children. This reduced the number of graduates in the high school for a time; but the public spirit which was aroused helped wonderfully to advance the interests of the schools, as the success of the project to build three new eight-roomed buildings in 1898 plainly showed. Up to this time there had been only four school buildings in the district: The High School, as it was called, although it was also used for grammar and primary pupils for many years; the Berkeley, built in 1868, and remodeled in 1892; the Center on Liberty Street; and the old Brookside, a small two-roomed building put up in 1868. The three new buildings, called Brookside, Fairview, and Watsessing, contrary to general expectation, were soon filled with scholars, and additions have since been added to each, making them fourteen-roomed schools. Because of the low price of material and labor at the time they were built they have proved an unusually good investment. Following this, as previously mentioned, the Center School, in 1893, was rebuilt with twelve rooms, and the Berkeley, in 1909, was doubled in size. All these schools are arranged in the most approved manner, with an efficient ventilating and heating system, large assembly halls, single seats and desks, and lighted by electricity. Finally a modern up-to-date building has been erected in Brookdale, upon the same plan and with the same improvements as the other schools, leaving the town in possession of six fine school buildings with all the latest appliances as follows: Berkeley, Brookside, Center, Brookdale, Fairview, and Watsessing. These are all for primary and grammar grades. One locality yet remains to be supplied, and for the Silver Lake School, for which a good lot has been purchased on Grove Street, there will be erected a modern building similar to the others.

When all these improvements for the lower grades had been completed, the demand for a new high school of sufficient size to accommodate all the scholars became irresistible. An appropriation was readily secured, and the land at the southwest corner of Broad Street and Belleville Avenue purchased. Plans were prepared by Charles Granville Jones, the architect since 1892 of all the school buildings, and a contract for its construction made. The building, now almost completed, is of stone and brick, four stories in height. When this building is occupied the high school will, for the first time in its history, be provided with all the necessary facilities for its work, including lecture, study, and recitation rooms; physical, chemical, and biological laboratories; manual training rooms, a gymnasium, and a large assembly hall to seat one thousand and capable of meeting all the requirements for public speaking, plays, graduating exercises, and serving various other uses. By far the

BLOOMFIELD HIGH SCHOOL (1912)

largest hall in the town, centrally located, having ample entrances and exits, and surrounded by practically a fireproof building, it is admirably adapted for public gatherings of a patriotic, political, or social character. Such a hall has long been needed and will be greatly appreciated.

We have reached the limits of our history. A closing word is all that is necessary. Bloomfield has no need to apologize for either her past or present educational history. In the early part of the past century she was the educational center of the cities and towns of the East. The students taught in her pay schools and academies adorned every profession, and were known throughout the land. No less distinguished are many of those later graduated from her free schools. It might be well for us to ask ourselves this question: Have we now reached the limit of achievement in school work? The answer will be, "By no means." Every system is productive of some good results. The pioneers, who sat at the feet of the schoolmaster in rooms lacking every comfort, came into close contact with men of learning and refinement, getting an inspiration which is often lacking in our larger classes. Again, the scholars of what might be called the academy period, when private schools were flourishing, had the advantage of meeting children of cultivated families brought together in such pay schools, and thus were made to feel that their opportunities should not be wasted. Classes were also small, and consequently better graded than is possible in the schools as at present carried on. With smaller classes, and more experienced teachers it would be possible to do better work.

The schools of to-day are for the millions. They

spread intelligence and patriotism among the masses as no other institution can. They have broader courses of study than those provided in earlier times, and are meeting the needs of boys and girls of many races and tongues. They will develop in a way to provide education for a complex civilization, which must have workers for the farms, the shops and the factories, as well as for the professions.

The record of Bloomfield has been one of consistent and carefully considered progress, step by step, almost without a break from the beginning. Recent history justifies the belief that the people of to-day are ready to meet the larger responsibilities, and the greater needs of the present, in the same spirit of generosity and courage as that exhibited by their predecessors, when with scanty means they opened their first school for the education of the community.

Bloomfield is justly proud of its large and well-organized school system, embracing eight schools, and presided over by more than one hundred teachers, having under their control about three thousand pupils, of whom over three hundred are in the High School. The time is fast approaching when people will realize that teaching is not a calling to be used merely as a stepping stone to something else more profitable. The self-sacrificing work done in the class-room will soon be better paid, and much of the talent now devoted to other labor will be attracted to the school-room, and the work of the teacher will rise to the dignity of a profession.

TRANSPORTATION

By Charles C. Ferguson

It is a long cry from the "gee-ha" of the ox driver to the "honk" of the automobile. Nearly two and one-half centuries intervene between the primitive and present day methods of transportation, and each progressive step has been in the direction of the elimination of time, the increase in carrying capacity; and, in the matter of passenger transportation, the promotion of the comfort and convenience of the traveling public.

The same successive steps in transition of methods of transportation that have contributed to the successful development of the United States, have all been experienced, and participated in, by the successive generations that have inhabited the particular section of the State of New Jersey and County of Essex, known as the Town of Bloomfield, and which, in this year 1912, is celebrating the Centennial anniversary of its organization as a municipality.

The Newark and Pompton Turnpike, in 1806; the Morris Canal, in 1831; the Newark and Bloomfield Railroad, in 1855; the street car line, in 1867, have been the essential features in the evolution of the superior transportation advantages that the present-day Bloomfielder enjoys as compared with those of the pioneer settlers.

A suspicion of witchcraft no longer applies to Mother Shipton's prophecy, "Carriages without horses shall run," and Tennyson's vision of "the heavens filled with commerce" is on the verge of becoming more than a poet's dream. Aerial navigation, however, belongs to a "higher realm" of transportation, and does not yet enter into the calculations of the practical business man of to-day.

It is but natural that a centennial period should arouse the reflective faculties, and a proper comparison and appreciation of what is now with what has been can only be reached by looking backward.

The problem of transportation in its earliest stage in this vicinity was an individual matter, the needs of commerce, and the traveling public did not enter into it. Few people traveled very far from home.

A religious compact was the foundation stone of Newark settlement in the latter half of the seventeenth century, and compulsory attendance at "town meetings" was a political obligation resting upon every settler, and the taking of grist to the mill was a necessity of life, and the transportation question resolved itself into a way to get to church, to town meeting, and to the mill.

The ox team and bolster wagon were the means of conveyance, and a trail along the line of least resistance was the primitive highway. The "old road to Newark," now Franklin Street, is conceived to be among the earliest of the trails or roads traversed by the pioneer settlers of Bloomfield, and the road through Belleville to Watsessing Dock on the Passaic River, the first highway of a commercial character.

When, in the course of events, in the early part of the eighteenth century, a business necessity, or a desire to see the world, prompted an early Bloomfielder to take a trip to New York, the method of transportation was by wagon to Watsessing Dock, and from thence by sloop

BLOOMFIELD, OLD AND NEW 103

down the Passaic. Schedule time did not figure in the trip. Wind and tide, and not steam or electricity, were the predominant factors in determining the time consumed in the trip.

Saw mills and grist mills first introduced the industrial element into transportation hereabouts, and the teamster, in consequence, became a factor in the industrial life of the community.

With the dawn of the nineteenth century, the industrial destiny of Newark and vicinity gave manifest evidence; and, with the developing of manufacturing, the commercial element in the transportation question became permanent. Among the first steps taken to meet the need was the planning and laying out of several important highways, and the year 1806 marks the first important move in this vicinity in the direction of a scientific development of the means of transportation; and that was the laying out and opening to travel of the Newark and Pompton Turnpike, now Bloomfield Avenue.

Bloomfield was represented in that enterprising move by two of its leading citizens, Israel Crane and John Dodd, who were active directors in the laying out and building of the road. From a commercial standpoint Bloomfield Turnpike was, at that time, as important as the opening of a new railroad would be to the present time. It proved a great accessory in the development of commerce. The freighter came on the scene, and great wagons laden with raw material from beyond the Delaware River, which was then the far West, traversed the avenue. It also increased facilities for getting farm products to market, and the wheel-wright and smithing industries flourished along the route. Wagon making, which was one of Bloomfield's early important industries, was stimulated by the opening of the turnpike.

While the turnpike was essentially a freighters' highway, it also introduced a new element into the transportation problem, in the line of passenger transportation. The traveling public was beginning to be a factor worthy of the attention of the man with an eye to business. The acme of rapid transit in the year 1800 was an eighteen-hour trip by stage from Jersey City to Philadelphia, with a ten dollar one-way rate of fair. Lines of stage conveyances were soon in active operation on all leading highways, and Bloomfield Center, now a trolley transfer point, was at one time an important stage post.

The year 1824 marked another progressive step in enlarging of transportation facilities, when the State Legislature granted a charter to the Morris Canal and Banking Company, to build a canal across the State from a point opposite Easton, Pa., on the Delaware River, to Newark, on the Passaic River; and later, in 1828, the charter was amended to enable the extension of the canal to Jersey City. Two distinctive features in the transportation business were embodied in the canal project: one was that it was purely an artificial artery of commerce, and the other that its construction was through the medium of aggregated capital. It marked a new and important era in transportation.

Manufacturing of various kinds, stage and express business, and other lines of commerce, had reached a point when iron, coal, wood, hay, and other heavy and bulky commodities were needed in larger quantities and at lower prices than could be obtained through the medium of the old time freighter and his wagon; but one of the prime factors that interested the attention of capitalists and scientific men to artificial navigation was the bringing of the product of the Pennsylvania coal fields to a profitable market, and had much to do with the conception and the direction of the Morris Canal project.

George McCullough, of Morristown, is credited with the origination of the then bold enterprise of constructing a canal from the Delaware to the Hudson River. The mountainous elevations between the two points were regarded as fatal objections to the project, and to overcome these Mr. McCullough adopted the expedient of inclined planes. Such planes, according to a commentary of the times, had never before been applied to boats of such magnitude, and to an operation so extensive.

Prizes were offered for the best ideas as to the construction of the proposed planes, and the successful competitor was Ephraim Morris of Bloomfield. His planes were adopted, and he was made general manager of the canal, a position he held from 1832 to 1843. One of the great planes of the canal is located here in Bloomfield, and has a vertical height of fifty-seven feet. From its upper end extends the long "seventeen-mile level," and old canalers west bound with their boats on Saturday evenings used to urge their mules forward to get over the Bloomfield plane before midnight Saturday night, in order to have the seventeen-mile level for a Sunday run, as the canal locks and planes were not operated in those days on Sunday, for the soul had not yet been squeezed out of corporations.

One day in November, 1832, there was a commotion in Bloomfield, and numerous people hurried to the plane, for five boats loaded with pig iron had left

Dover, and were making a trial trip of the canal, and a test of the planes and locks. The ease and facility with which the boats were passed over the plane astonished the spectators, and the great achievement was the town topic for many days.

Water was turned into the canal for the purpose of regular operations in April, 1832; but a break in a dyke near Easton delayed the beginning of traffic for another month. The first boat to reach Newark was the "Walk in the Water" with a consignment for the Stephens & Condit Transportation Company.

Another red letter day in canal history was the arrival of two boats loaded with coal from Mauch Chunk, Pa. Enterprising coal dealers urged the people to lay in an early supply, as canal navigation would close in winter time. Canal boats rapidly increased in number, and the freight tonnage reached enormous totals for the times.

The canal traversed Bloomfield through the longest direction, and the town was an important point on the canal, and the coal yards here supplied a very extensive territory, and in that section of the town known as the plane a business center of a considerable importance was built up.

A well-known Bloomfielder, Jacob F. Randolph, was president of the Canal Company a number of years.

The canal was used in a limited way for passenger travel, and the packet boat "Marion Colden," drawn by three horses, was a "flyer" of the times. It made daily trips (Sundays excepted) between Newark and Passaic. The fare to Bloomfield was twenty-five cents, and to Passaic, fifty cents. It was a popular excursion boat. At Passaic, then called Acquackanonck, excursionists had an opportunity to ride on the new railroad, now the Erie Railroad, to Paterson. Ephraim Morris was the builder of the packet boat.

In 1871 the Morris Canal was transferred under a perpetual lease to the Lehigh Valley Railroad, and not many years after that it became defunct as an artery of transportation. For many years now it has been regarded as a detriment to the town, but there are indications of a transformation in which the canal route will again become a useful and valuable factor as a transportation route of the most approved rapid transit character.

In noting the development of the process of transportation from the latter part of the seventeenth century to the first half of the nineteenth century, the first personages who appeared upon the scene were the pioneer settlers, with whom the problem of transportation involved only their individual needs and convenience. The industrial element was introduced with the appearance of the teamster, whose livelihood was earned in the transporting of logs to saw mills. Next appeared a more dignified and romantic personage, in the freighter, whose business was the transportation of raw materials and merchandise between the manufacturer in the city and the country merchants in the remote district. Next followed the independent canal boat captain, and the application of science and art to transportation.

Canals, however, were not long equal to the demands of commerce in the line of transportation.

Science and art had applied their efforts to further improvement of means of travel and freight communication, and capital was ready to back up and further any device that promised to meet the expanding needs.

Science and art brought forth the steam locomotive and the railroad, and capital busied itself in the exploitations of the new device; and the present day and generation is witness to the marvelous results since 1830, when the State Legislature chartered the first railroad enterprise in New Jersey, the Camden and Amboy Railroad, which soon became a power both in the industrial and political interests of the State.

The Morris and Essex Railroad, incorporated in 1835, brought the railroad in close proximity to Bloomfield. The Morris and Essex, in the early years of its operation, did not stand as now in the front rank as a passenger line. Cars were diverted from the terminus of the main line at Newark, and drawn by horses down Broad and Center streets to the Center Street station of the New Jersey Railroad and Transportation Company, and were thence run over that company's tracks to Jersey city.

In 1855 the road was extended to East Newark, and a more perfect junction made with the New Jersey Railroad.

In 1860 the Hoboken Land and Improvement Company obtained a charter for a railroad connecting Newark with Hoboken, and the Morris and Essex trains were then run direct to Hoboken through the Bergen tunnel of the New York and Erie Railroad.

In 1868, the Morris and Essex and its branches were leased to the Delaware, Lackawanna and Western Railroad and a new and independent tunnel was completed in 1877.

Old Bloomfield has suffered the reproach of slowness, but history bears evidence that the appellation was a misnomer. In the adoption and application of improved processes of transportation Bloomfield enterprise has made a record to be proud of. It was Bloomfield brains and capital that were influential in the opening of the Newark and Pompton Turnpike, among the first commercial highways in Essex County. It was Bloomfield ingenuity that surmounted the engineering difficulties in the way of the construction of the Morris Canal, and that new and improved process of transportation, the railroad, had scarcely been demonstrated a success when Bloomfield enterprise and Bloomfield capital took up the idea and gave their town the benefit of their work in the construction of the Newark and Bloomfield Railroad, chartered on March 26, 1852, and completed to Bloomfield in December, 1855, and West Bloomfield, now Montclair, in 1856.

The incorporators, when the charter was obtained, were Zenas S. Crane, Dr. Joseph A. Davis, Ira Dodd, Grant J. Wheeler, Robert L. Cook, David Oakes, David Conger, William S. Morris, and Warren S. Baldwin.

Dr. Joseph A. Davis was the first president of the railroad, and an influential factor in furthering its construction. He took up the first spadeful of earth, when the construction work was started, at a point near Clark Street. The occasion was one of some note, and the Rev. Job Halsey of Montclair delivered an oration to the assembled people. When the road was first projected the promoters opened negotiations with the New Jersey Railroad Company for a New York connection, but the negotiations did not prove satisfactory, and final arrangements were made with the Morris and Essex Railroad Company for building the road. The Morris and Essex Company furnished $55,000 of the capital stock, and $50,000 was subscribed, mostly in

Bloomfield. The road was subsequently leased to the Morris and Essex Company on a guarantee of 6 per cent. interest on its stock of $103,850, less than half the sum that the Lackawanna Company spent in improvements at the Bloomfield and Watsessing station in 1911.

Ira Dodd, of Bloomfield, was the first superintendent of the Newark and Bloomfield Railroad.

Three trains each way daily filled the requirements of the traveling public. When the road first opened New York passengers changed cars at Roseville. Some of the trains were mixed trains, made up of freight and passenger cars, and passengers waited patiently while the locomotive drilled freight cars on the siding. The Glenwood Avenue station, the first built along the line of the road, did duty until November, 1911. The first Watsessing station was called Doddtown, and was located at Willow Street. A bell on a tower at the Glenwood Avenue station warned the people of the approach of a train.

The first conductor on the road was Samuel Arbuthnot, afterward ticket agent at the Glenwood Avenue station. Charles Willetts was the first engineer. Charles Corby was promoted from baggage master to conductor, and served the company many years. Peter Tronson was many years an engineer on the road, and James Patrick and Edward Cain of Montclair were among the early brakemen.

The important position of legal counsel for the company was held by the Honorable Amzi Dodd, who conducted the negotiations with landowners for the right of way. With the advent of railroads the traveling public became an element in transportation matters, and the Newark and Bloomfield Railroad management has always had before it the constant problem of keeping pace with the demands upon it by its ever-increasing passenger travel, and the daily passenger traffic now exceeds that of a month in 1860.

The Glen Ridge station was opened in 1860, and through trains to New York were run in 1865.

The marvelous growth of the patronage of the Newark and Bloomfield Railroad gave rise in 1867 to another railroad enterprise, when a charter was granted to the New York, Montclair and Greenwood Lake Railroad, and the building of the road was completed in 1872. Robert M. Henning, Julius H. Pratt, and Henry C. Spaulding were active promoters of the new railroad.

This new road was one of the causes of the division between Bloomfield and Montclair. The promoters sought to have the township bonded to build the road. The proposition was stoutly resisted here, and the matter was discussed at a stormy town meeting. A bonding act was passed by the Legislature, but Bloomfield was exempted from its provisions. Montclair was bonded for $200,000.

A notable day in Bloomfield was an incident in connection with the construction of the New York and Greenwood Lake Railroad. A dispute arose over the construction of the Broad Street bridge, and the ringing of the old First Church bell was the signal for the citizens to rush to the scene of trouble and resist an invasion of the public rights. The sheriff of the county appeared on the scene and dispersed the assemblage.

The New York and Greenwood Lake Railroad and its Orange Branch, which traverses the southern portion of the town, is now operated by the Erie Railroad Company, and under that company's mangement is giving the town a good passenger service between here and New York, and has built up a large commuting patronage.

The Orange branch, as yet, is chiefly a freight road, and carries an immense tonnage annually.

Following the steam railroads, the next innovation in transportation here was the introduction of the street railway, designed for passenger service solely. The increase in population and the need of more direct and frequent communication with Newark was the stimulus for an embarkation in the street railway business by a number of local capitalists; and the Newark, Bloomfield and Montclair Horse Car Railroad Company was chartered in 1867.

The road was originally built from near the cemetery gate on Belleville Avenue, where the car barn was located, and along Belleville Avenue to Broad Street, along the west side of the park to Franklin Street to Newark Avenue, then a new street just opened as a part of the railway scheme, and along Newark Avenue to the north end of Mt. Prospect Avenue, thence to Bloomfield Avenue, to Belleville Avenue to Broad Street, Newark.

The route proved too roundabout, and too much time was consumed in the trip, and the new enterprise was not a success. If the present electrical equipment of street railroads had been in vogue then, the result would have been different, and Newark Avenue may yet fulfill its original design as a street railway route. In 1876 the street railway passed into the hands of the Newark and Bloomfield Street Railway Company, and the tracks were laid on Bloomfield Avenue, a more direct route.

The Bloomfield line figured in the various corporate changes that have marked the history of street railway transportation, and out of which the Public Service railway eventually evolved, and which is now one of the leading street car railway companies of the country.

In 1890 or thereabouts there was made an addition in the street railway service of the town by the building of the Orange and Bloomfield Railroad, now known as the cross-town branch of the Public Service Company. It was promoted and built by Francis M. Eppley of Orange, and was considered at the time a risky venture, but subsequent developments have demonstrated that Mr. Eppley correctly diagnosed the future prospects of the line.

Automobile transportation in Bloomfield, in so far as passengers are concerned, has been confined to the transportation of the individual and members of his family and guests. There is a possibility, however, that passenger service by automobile service may yet be added to the transportation facilities of the town.

Unless the street railways monopolize such important thoroughfares as Washington Street and Montgomery Street, public auto service may yet traverse those streets. The commercial auto, for express and delivery service, is now a familiar sight in the streets.

Bloomfield railroad train service in 1856 consisted of about three trains each way between here and Newark by way of the Newark and Bloomfield Railroad.

In this year of 1912 the train service consists of thirty-two trains each way between here and New York on the Lackawanna Railroad, nineteen each way on the New York and Greenwood Lake Railroad, and eight each way on the Watchung Railroad, a total of one hundred and eighteen passenger trains on week days, and a large number of Sunday trains. Freight transportation is independent of passenger service, and about eighteen long trains of freight pass daily over the railroad lines here, and a large part of the cargo of those trains is either delivered or collected in Bloomfield. The number of trolley cars that traverse the town runs into the hundreds daily.

Bloomfield's present position in the matter of transportation facilities, both as to passenger travel and express and freight delivery, is a good one. The steam railroads that traverse the town are branches of two of the country's great trunk lines, the Lackawanna and the Erie.

At Newark, only four miles away, the Bloomfielder can get aboard the Lackawanna main line trains for all points west, and at Jersey City the New York and Greenwood Lake makes a similar connection with the Erie main line. Tickets to almost any point in the country are on sale at the local ticket offices, and two of the leading express companies, the United States and the Wells Fargo, afford all the express services relative to travel. It is only a short ride by trolley to the Pennsylvania Railroad station in Newark, where trains can be boarded for all southern and southwestern points.

For short trips, the Public Service Corporation's trolley lines have the town well connected up with all the principal towns within a radius of twenty miles. The Bloomfielder who, in 1850, got into a stage at the center and rode to the Center Street station of the New Jersey Railroad in Newark, and from thence went by train to New York, would be amazed at the transporta-

BLOOMFIELD, OLD AND NEW 115

tion improvements of the past fifty years could he revisit his former terrestrial abode. The patron of the old Newark and Bloomfield Horse Car Line, whose heart ached with sympathy for the poor horses that tugged the loaded cars, would be astonished and delighted with present-day trolley cars. The ancient mariner whose craft plied the Morris Canal and whose bugle signal to get the lock ready was once a familiar sound, would be the only one likely to mourn over a decadence in commercial activity as he contemplated upon the present deserted and neglected conditions of that once famous and active commercial highway.

Progressiveness in transportation facilities has been one of the foundation stones of Bloomfield's prosperity, and a retrospective glance at the successive steps in the progression reveals the elements of a self-made town. Let those of the present generation, who thoughtlessly hurl reproaches of slowness and old fogyism at the old-time Bloomfielders, stop and compare records. Let them point out where within the past forty years they themselves have taken one initiative step toward effecting any improvements in transportation facilities. Let them pause and reflect upon it, that the Cranes and the Dodds of Bloomfield were leading factors in the promotion of the first commercial highway that traversed this section, namely the Newark and Pompton Turnpike. Let it not be overlooked that nearly one hundred years ago it was the ingenuity of Ephraim Morris, an honored Bloomfielder, that contributed to the successful operation of the Morris Canal.

A little over half a century ago the energy, the enterprise and the capital of the Davis's, the Dodd's, the Baldwin's, and the Oakes's, all old-time honored Bloomfield names, gave the town its first railroad. The same names appear also in the first efforts to give the town a street railway system.

Citizens who take the initiative in securing improvements for their town cannot truthfully be dubbed slow and unprogressive, and it is but fitting in this Centennial year that the services Bloomfield's former leading citizens rendered for their own town be held up to the light of the present day, and that a fitting respect be paid to the memory of the self-made men, who by their personal enterprise and energy gave the town a history to be proud of.

Transportation facilities, marvelous as they are now as compared with a half century ago, are yet in a transitory stage, and the future has wonders in store for the generations to come.

Art and science, stimulants of genius, are as busy to-day as of yore, when they brought forth the canal as a morsel of their handiwork, and followed it with a greater wonder, the steam locomotive. Steam displaced water power as a motor force, and is in turn being displaced by a more subtle and powerful force, electricity. It was a mental possibility to calculate the dynamics of steam power, but the possibilities of electric energy are incalculable, and it may be said inconceivable.

It is possible that the next generation of Bloomfielders may see steam power supplanted by electric energy in all the railroads that traverse the town. There is no question but that transportation facilities will be increased and improved. The Lackawanna Railroad Company, by its expenditure of hundreds of thousands of dollars here on the improvements in its line, has given unmistakable evidence of its faith in the future.

BLOOMFIELD, OLD AND NEW

There is a demand for extensions of the trolley lines, and the demand must and will be met.

The historians of the first century of the life of the municipality of Bloomfield have had a marvelous story to tell of development and progress, and those whose lot it may be to record the annals of the second centennial may have a still more wonderful tale to relate. We of the present day are inclined to self-congratulation and compliment that we have lived in and contributed to an age of progress. We can complacently smile upon the enthusiasm of those who thought the acme of progress had been reached when the Morris Canal was opened for traffic. Will the historians of the second centennial smile upon our egotism and compare their transportation facilities with ours, in the sense and to the degree that we compare ours with the ox team and bolster wagon of the pioneer Bloomfielder?

THE HISTORY OF THE CHURCHES

By George Louis Curtis

THE section of New Jersey of which Bloomfield is a part was settled over two centuries ago by men of deeply religious convictions, and the community has retained to the present day the impress made by those early colonists. The town is well provided with churches, attendance upon their services is general, and their influence is felt in a marked degree. The church life is remarkably harmonious, and marked by a spirit of cordial cooperation rather than competition. Six of the leading churches, of the Presbyterian, Baptist, Methodist and Congregational denominations, are united in what is known as the Bloomfield Evangelical Union, holding quarterly union services and working together for the public welfare. The churches are mentioned here in the order of their organization.

The first church to be organized was Presbyterian. For many years the early settlers of this locality were obliged to go several miles for worship, attending either the Newark Church or the Second Presbyterian Church of the Township, now known as the First Presbyterian Church of Orange. In 1794 members of a society that had been meeting in school or private houses, in what was then called Wardsesson, petitioned the Presbytery of New York for organization as the Third Presbyterian Congregation in the Township of Newark. This request was granted on July 23, 1794. On October 24, 1796, trustees who had been elected at a public meeting held on August 9th, in the house of Joseph Davis on Franklin Street, met in the same place and assumed the name of "The Trustees of the Presbyterian Society of Bloomfield." Three days later a subscription was begun for the erection of a church edifice which was placed on a knoll facing the field that soon became the "Common" or "Green." For many years this was the only place of worship in the community, and the center of its religious life. The building was constructed of brown free-stone, and the mortar which cemented it was purchased with the gift of $140 made by General, afterward Governor, Joseph Bloomfield, in whose honor the new name for church and town had been chosen. Isaac Dodd, Ephraim Morris, Joseph Crane and Simeon Baldwin were elected deacons in 1798, and served as the first church officers. "The Church on the Green," now known as the First Presbyterian Church, after more than a century of service, still fulfills its original purpose, as it bids fair to do for many years to come.

So much of the early history of the town is connected with that of this church that the reader is referred to Chapter First of this volume for details down to the year 1810, when the pastorate of Rev. Abel Jackson, its first minister, terminated. The ministerial succession has been as follows:

Rev. Abel Jackson 1800-1810
Rev. Cyrus Gildersleeve 1812-1818
Rev. Gideon N. Judd, D.D 1820-1834
Rev. Ebenezer Seymour 1834-1847
Rev. George Duffield, D.D 1847-1851
Rev. James M. Sherwood, D.D 1852-1858
Rev. Ellis J. Newlin, D.D 1859-1863
Rev. Charles E. Knox, D.D 1864-1873
Rev. Henry W. Ballantine, D.D 1874-1894
Rev. James Beveridge Lee, D.D 1894-1899
Rev. George Louis Curtis, D.D., installed in April, 1900

Great changes have occurred during these hundred years. Candles have given way to electricity. The posts and chain around the "Common" have disappeared since the "Park" was graded under the engineering eye of Dr. Ballantine. The original structure has been lengthened, and the Sunday-school room has been added. A new tower was built, and a clock with a Westminster chime of bells, the gift of members of the Davis family, was added in 1896, at the time of the centennial celebration. A fine new organ with chimes was installed in October, 1911. The Parish House was erected in 1840. This was designed not only for devotional meetings, but also for those of the "Young Men's Lyceum," whose literary exercises and debates were held there, and for town meetings and elections as well, and for many years it was so used.

The change from an "Associate" or independent Presbyterian Church following the Congregational usage, under Rev. Abel Jackson, to its perfected organization as a Presbyterian Church was made in 1812, soon after the installation of Rev. Cyrus Gildersleeve. It is interesting to note that this second pastor, on removing from the South, brought his slaves with him; but slaves were held by other Bloomfielders also at that time. Dr. Judd's pastorate was marked by several great revivals of religion. Dr. George Duffield is widely known as the author of "Stand up, stand up for Jesus." Dr. Charles E. Knox, during whose pastorate the colony left to form the Westminster Presbyterian Church, resigned to become the first president of the German Theological School of Newark, located in this town. The membership of the church is now 778, and of the Sunday-school, 282.

PRESBYTERIAN CHURCH, LECTURE ROOM AND STONE SCHOOLHOUSE (1840)

The Broughton Memorial Chapel is an outlying station of "The Old First Church," doing the same work, and open to all, regardless of denomination. In 1870 an organization was formed by young men of the First and Westminster churches for Christian work among the boatmen on the Morris Canal. A building known as "Hope Chapel" was completed in February, 1871, in which a Sunday-school was started. Preaching was soon suspended, owing to decreasing business on the canal; but the Sunday-school flourished. The present building on Bay Avenue was dedicated in November, 1899. In 1907 an addition was built, more land was purchased, a pool-table and bowling alleys were installed in the basement, making the total outlay about $10,000.

The first superintendent was N. B. Collins, who had been active in procuring the land and securing subscriptions for the erection of the first building. His term of service lasted about six months. His successors have been the following: John F. Seymour, 1871 to 1876; William A. Baldwin, 1876 to 1881; John F. Woodhull, 1881 to 1882; John G. Broughton, 1882 to 1894; William A. Baldwin, 1894 to the present time.

The present name was given in honor of John G. Broughton, whose faithful service as superintendent for twelve years, supplemented by his genial manner, drew hosts of friends about him, and endeared him to the whole community. The present number of officers, teachers and pupils is 203.

Sunday evening services were begun in February, 1908. Walter S. Hertzog, of Union Theological Seminary, New York City, was the preacher for the first winter. C. Henry Holbrook, now a missionary in Turkey, succeeded him for two years. The services are now in charge of Laurence Fenninger, who began his work in October, 1910.

THE BROOKDALE REFORMED (DUTCH) CHURCH is one of the oldest churches of a wide region. The meetings from which it grew began in 1795, when this section was known as Stone House Plains. The Reformed Church at Acquackanonck (Passaic), organized in 1691, the First Presbyterian Church of Bloomfield, organized in 1696, and the Reformed Church at Second River (Belleville), organized in 1700, were then the only churches within a radius of over six miles. The Rev. Peter Stryker, pastor of the church at Second River, began the preaching services, the meeting-house, it is said, being improvised out of a barn. By direction of the Classis of Bergen he organized the church in October, 1801, becoming its founder and first pastor while continuing to serve the church at Second River. For half a century the outskirts of the parish extended to Franklin, Athenia, beyond the Great Notch, and "over the mountain," that is, to Cedar Grove.

The first consistory was composed of Yellis Mandeville and Walling Egberts, elders, and Francis Speer, deacon. The church edifice, a stone structure, was built and used as a place of worship in 1802, but was not finished until later. It was only forty by fifty feet, and was without tower or bell. The land was the gift of Abram Garrabrant. The building was rebuilt in 1857. The steeple and bell were added through the generosity of James G. Speer, of Cincinnati, a former member, in 1860. After having been burned, the building was again rebuilt and enlarged in 1910. The Rev. Peter Stryker served as stated supply and pastor from 1801 to 1826. He has been succeeded by the following ministers of the

Reformed (Dutch) Church: The Rev. Messrs. John G. Tarbell, Alexander C. Hillman, Eben S. Hammond, William Thompson, Robert A. Quinn, John A. Liddell, John Wiseman, Peter Stryker Talmage, Benjamin T. Statesir, John Kershaw, Jacob O. Van Fleet, William G. E. See, William E. Bogardus and Charles E. Waldron. The present pastor, the Rev. Charles E. Waldron, was installed in 1909. The present membership of the church is 85, and of the Sunday-school, 105.

THE PARK METHODIST EPISCOPAL CHURCH was the third church to be organized in Bloomfield, having been started in 1832. The Rev. Benjamin Day was its first pastor. In the list of his successors are several names of unusual distinction, including those of Bishop Henry Spellmeyer and Rev. Jesse Lyman Hurlbut, D.D., the present District Superintendent of Newark Conference. The church building, of stuccoed brick, erected on the west side of the "Green" in 1853, was enlarged in 1881, during the pastorate of Rev. Richard Harcourt.

The Watsessing Methodist Episcopal Church was started by this church in 1871, Dr. Stephen L. Baldwin being the pastor of the Park Church at that time.

The chapel was built during the pastorate of Rev. D. R. Lowry, 1882-5. Rev. John Ogden Winner, the present pastor, was installed in April, 1910. A beautiful and commodious parish house has lately been added, and was dedicated December 10, 1911. The material is light-colored brick, with stone columns and trimmings. The interior is attractively arranged and furnished, and it is fully equipped for social and Sabbath-school purposes, and for all forms of present-day service.

The following is a list of the pastors from 1832 to

1912: The Rev. Messrs. Benjamin Day, Walter Burrows, Isaac N. Felch, J. I. Morrow, G. K. Snyder, D. F. Reed, John Scarlett, W. W. Voorhees, S. H. Opdyke, George Winson, John S. Swain, A. S. Compton, J. R. Adams, Stacy W. Hilliard, Stephen L. Baldwin, Henry Spellmeyer, E. W. Burr, W. L. Hoagland, Richard Harcourt, Daniel R. Lowrie, Albert Mann, Jr., J. A. Monroe, R. B. Collins, R. M. Aylsworth, J. G. Johnston, C. S. Woodruff, Jesse Lyman Hurlbut, Nathaniel Brooks, and John Ogden Winner.

THE FIRST BAPTIST CHURCH occupies the corner of Franklin and Washington streets, and the organization dates from November 25, 1851. The present building was erected in 1911, and its Sabbath-school building in 1891. Rev. John D. Meeson was the first pastor. He has been succeeded by Rev. James H. Pratt, Rev. Henry F. Smith, Rev. W. F. Stubbert, D.D., Rev. Ezra D. Simons, Rev. Charles A. Cook, Rev. Fred W. Buis, and Rev. Henry S. Potter, S.T.D. The present pastor, Dr. Potter, was installed June 1, 1907. The present membership of the church is 565, while the Sunday-school, the largest in town, has an enrollment, including the Home Department and Cradle Roll, of 865.

The Silver Lake Chapel, in which services had been conducted by the First Baptist Church for several years, was recently burned, but will soon be rebuilt in another location. It is worthy of note that the church was organized with a constituent membership of thirteen, and none of them wealthy; yet they immediately purchased the large corner lot and built what was then a fine brick structure, and dedicated it free of debt within nineteen months. The present parsonage was purchased in 1907. In 1903 the W. C. T. U. Hall adjoining the church property was purchased and at a considerable expense fitted up for use as a hall for the Primary Department of the Bible School.

In 1910 the stately old brick building that had stood on that prominent site for nearly sixty years was razed, and in its place a larger modern building was erected, constructed of West Townsend (Mass.) granite, at an outlay, including furnishings, of over seventy thousand dollars. Worthy of special note is the large modern "Memorial" organ with twenty-six speaking registers. The property of the church is valued at $125,000.

In 1901 the church celebrated its fiftieth anniversary with elaborate festivities, and issued a beautiful volume illustrating the progress of a half century.

Mr. Frank B. Stone, superintendent of the Bible School, has filled that office for thirty years.

The spirit of this church in relation to country and community is shown by the fact that out of sixty male members at the outbreak of the Civil War, twenty entered the United States Army.

THE GERMAN PRESBYTERIAN CHURCH, situated on Park Avenue, and of which the Rev. Remi J. Buttinghausen is pastor, was organized January 1, 1855. The present building was erected in 1895. The church's half-century and more of history may be summarized as follows:

On the first day of January, 1857, a group of thirty-seven Christian men and women of German birth gathered at the chapel of the First Presbyterian Church of Bloomfield to be organized into a church in accordance with the principles and doctrines of the Presbyterian Church, and to be known as the German Presbyterian

Church of Bloomfield, N. J. Of the thirty-seven original members, all but three have departed this life. Those still living and connected with the church are Jacob Fornoff, Henry Bickler and Elizabeth Metz.

For a number of years the little flock met at the chapel of the First Presbyterian Church, whose pastor, the Rev. Dr. Sherwood, took a very warm interest in the new movement.

During this time the church had no regular pastor, the pulpit being supplied by the Rev. Mr. Thebrath of Newark, N. J., and Christian Wisner, a student at the Union Theological Seminary of New York. On the 29th day of April, 1864, Mr. Wisner was ordained to the Christian ministry and installed as the first regular pastor of the church. In the following year the first church building was erected at a cost of $4,600.

The Rev. Mr. Wisner remained but a few years as pastor of the church, and his work was continued by the Rev. John Enslin, who, after serving the church faithfully for twenty-two years, departed this life on the 12th day of April, 1890. During his ministry the parsonage was erected.

In the fall of the year 1890, the Rev. Henry Seibert, D.D., was installed as pastor of the church. In 1895 the present house of worship was built.

In 1899 Dr. Seibert accepted the call extended to him by the First German Presbyterian Church of Newark, N. J. The pastoral work of the Bloomfield church was then entrusted to the late Rev. Otto Zesch, D.D., who served it from 1899 to 1902. Since the spring of 1903 the Rev. R. J. Buttinghausen has been the pastor.

The church has a membership of 210. There are 250 scholars and teachers connected with the Sunday-school, of which Mr. Carl Seibert is the superintendent.

CHRIST (EPISCOPAL) CHURCH in Bloomfield and Glen Ridge stands on the dividing line between those two municipalities, on the corner of Bloomfield and Park avenues. The organization dates from 1858, when a number of English families living in the town of Bloomfield, which at that time included Glen Ridge and Montclair (known as West Bloomfield), requested Rev. Henry Beers Sherman, then rector of Christ Church, Belleville, to conduct services for them after the order of the Church of England. The services were at first held in a private house on Franklin Street, then in a public house known as Archdeacon's Hotel, and later in an upper room known as Union Hall on the northwest corner of Washington and Glenwood avenues.

The parish organization was formed October 4, 1858, and Rev. Henry Marsh was chosen the first rector.

The first church edifice was erected on Liberty Street, and consecrated June 23, 1861. This, together with the adjoining parish house, was destroyed by fire on the night of January 11, 1893. Meantime a movement looking toward the establishment of a new parish in Glen Ridge had resulted in the formation of a society called the St. Mark's Society. This Society united with Christ Church after the fire, and the present site was chosen for the new church as more convenient for ministering to the needs of the greatly enlarged parish overlapping both towns.

The cost of the new church and parish house, including organ, furniture, etc., was approximately $40,000, which, however, does not represent the actual value of the buildings, even at the time of erection. The interior stone was the last stone quarried from the Glen Ridge quarry on Bloomfield Avenue, on the spot since filled in and now used as the playground of the Glen Ridge Public School. The exterior stone was the first taken from a quarry at Pompton. The rectory adjoining the church was completed in October, 1905.

St. Luke's Church, Montclair, is the outgrowth of a Mission started during the rectorship of Rev. Mr. Marsh in Bloomfield, and is the eldest of four daughters of Christ Church. A Sunday-school started in Franklin, while Dr. Carter was rector here, has since developed into the parish of Grace Church, Nutley. The Chapel erected in Watsessing during the same period was the beginning of the new parish of St. Paul's Church, East Orange. A Mission on Montgomery Avenue, started by Christ Church in 1901, has since become the Church of the Ascension.

The list of rectors of Christ Church is as follows:

Rev. Henry Marsh 1860-1863
Rev. Charles Ritter 1863-1864
Rev. William A. W. Maybin..............1864-1865
Rev. Albert Zabriskie Gray...............1865-1868
Rev. William H. Carter, D.D.............1869-1872
Rev. T. Jefferson Danner 1872-1877
Rev. William G. Farrington, D.D.........1877-1889
Rev. Robert S. Carlin...................1889-1891
Rev. Edward Augustine White, D.C.L.,
      Elected January 11, 1892

The main growth of Christ Church thus far has taken place during the rectorship of Dr. White, the twentieth anniversary of whose installation was celebrated in January, 1912. Dr. White is also a recognized authority stone was the last stone quarried from the Glen Ridge quarry on Bloomfield Avenue, on the spot since filled in and now used as the playground of the Glen Ridge Public School. The exterior stone was the first taken from a quarry at Pompton. The rectory adjoining the church was completed in October, 1905.

St. Luke's Church, Montclair, is the outgrowth of a Mission started during the rectorship of Rev. Mr. Marsh in Bloomfield, and is the eldest of four daughters of Christ Church. A Sunday-school started in Franklin, while Dr. Carter was rector here, has since developed into the parish of Grace Church, Nutley. The Chapel erected in Watsessing during the same period was the beginning of the new parish of St. Paul's Church, East Orange. A Mission on Montgomery Avenue, started by Christ Church in 1901, has since become the Church of the Ascension.

The list of rectors of Christ Church is as follows:

Rev. Henry Marsh 1860-1863
Rev. Charles Ritter 1863-1864
Rev. William A. W. Maybin............. 1864-1865
Rev. Albert Zabriskie Gray.............. 1865-1868
Rev. William H. Carter, D.D............ 1869-1872
Rev. T. Jefferson Danner 1872-1877
Rev. William G. Farrington, D.D......... 1877-1889
Rev. Robert S. Carlin................... 1889-1891
Rev. Edward Augustine White, D.C.L.,
              Elected January 11, 1892

The main growth of Christ Church thus far has taken place during the rectorship of Dr. White, the twentieth anniversary of whose installation was celebrated in January, 1912. Dr. White is also a recognized authority on canon law in the Protestant Episcopal Church. The present communicant membership of the church is about 700, and that of the Sunday-school, 250. Rev. George G. Daland is Curate and Choirmaster-organist. The wardens are Messrs. Thaddeus S. Genin and William H. Sayre. The Reception Committee, of which Mr. Talbot Root is president, is one of the strongest and most effective organizations of men in the Diocese of Newark.

THE WESTMINSTER PRESBYTERIAN CHURCH, which occupies a group of handsome buildings on Franklin and Fremont streets, was originally made up of a colony from "the Old First Church." Increased membership and lack of adequate accommodation were the reasons leading to the establishment of the new organization, and Rev. Charles E. Knox, D.D., then pastor of the old church, earnestly used his influence in its favor.

The movement was initiated at a meeting held on June 25, 1869, when fifty-one persons signified their intention of becoming identified with the new enterprise. The first service was held on July 11, 1869, in the Academy (now the German Theological School), with eighty-two persons present, and Dr. Knox preaching the sermon. Eucleian Hall, at the corner of Washington and Glenwood avenues, was afterward secured as a meeting-place, and Rev. Duncan Kennedy, D.D., of Troy, N. Y., was engaged as stated supply. The new organization was formally constituted by Presbytery into a church on January 7, 1870, with sixty-seven charter members.

The first officers of the church elected were Moses M. Bradley and Coll J. Turner, elders; Robert J. Beach and Frederick Crane, deacons. The first board of trustees, chosen at a meeting of the parish January

21st, was composed of Rev. J. D. Gallagher, Daniel H. Temple, Harry E. Richards, Jason Crane, Phineas J. Ward and Edward A. Bliss.

On May 27, 1870, Rev. Duncan Kennedy, D.D., was called to become the first pastor of the church. A chapel was erected on Fremont Street, and the installation and dedicatory services were both held on September 30, 1870. Dr. Kennedy resigned in 1881 owing to the infirmities of age, and was succeeded in 1882 by Rev. Samuel W. Duffield, who died in the harness on May 12, 1887. Mr. Duffield was a man of literary ability, an authority on hymnology, and the author of two volumes on English Hymns and Latin Hymns. Rev. George A. Paull, D.D., followed in a pastorate extending over eighteen years, a period of steady growth and large expansion for the church. Rev. William T. Wilcox, D.D., the present pastor, was installed on May 27, 1907.

The new church building was dedicated April 12, 1892. The chapel, after having been partially destroyed by fire and rebuilt, was removed in 1901 to the corner of Liberty Street and Austin Place, and is now used for worship by St. John's German Lutheran Church. The beautiful Jarvie Memorial, of brown stone, with its spacious hall, parlors, gymnasium, etc., was erected in 1902 by James N. Jarvie in memory of his parents, and presented to the church of which they had been among the original members. This building also houses the Jarvie Memorial Public Library, containing some 14,000 well-selected volumes on all subjects, and with commodious reading-rooms and all the appliances of a thoroughly modern reference and circulating library. In completeness and elegance of equipment this church is now probably without a superior in the State.

Twenty-one families withdrew in 1888-9 to form the Glen Ridge Congregational Church; but the migration reduced the membership only temporarily. The present membership of the church is about 605, and of the Sunday-school, 425.

Montgomery Chapel, located just across the Belleville line, is maintained by Westminster Church. It is the result of Sunday-school work that began with a school under the care of Erasmus D. Willes, April 23, 1826. The sessions of the school were held at the Quarries, and only during the summer months.

The superintendents since that time have been J. Vants, Gilbert Combs, Isaac N. Dodd, Elias Osborne, L. W. Hones, Miss Jennie A. Osborne, Richard Handy, and W. S. Phraner. Mr. Phraner took charge of the school September 15, 1891. At that time the place of meeting was the old school-house situated on Montgomery Street, in the Soho section of Belleville. In October, 1895, the present chapel was started, and was completed and dedicated March 15, 1896. Since that time a primary-room, library, gymnasium, bowling alleys, pipe-organ and other conveniences have been gradually added. The present enrollment of the school is 205. The Sabbath-school meets on Sunday afternoons at 3.15. A preaching service is also held every Sabbath evening at 8 o'clock. The building is open through the week, and is used and appreciated by those who live in that neighborhood.

Although non-sectarian, the school depends almost entirely for its support on Westminster Church. The property, estimated at $14,000, is held under a deed of trust by three trustees, Frederick Crane, Joseph M. Williams, and W. S. Phraner.

THE WATSESSING METHODIST EPISCOPAL CHURCH is situated on Lawrence Street, corner of Dodd Street, East Orange, in the heart of the section originally known as Wardsesson. It was organized in 1871, and Rev. W. B. Rulison was the first pastor. Andrew Ellor and his wife, Ann Ellor, were the prime movers in the organization of the church, under the supervision of Rev. Stephen L. Baldwin, then pastor of the Park Methodist Episcopal Church of Bloomfield. A Sunday-school was organized in Butterworth's Hall about 1871. Ebenezer E. Francis was its first superintendent, and was succeeded by Andrew Ellor.

The first building, now known as the chapel, was erected in the winter of 1871-2, and was opened in February, 1872. During the pastorate of Rev. C. C. Winans the present church edifice was built in the winter of 1894-5, and was opened in May, 1895.

The list of pastors in the history of the church thus far is as follows: Rev. Messrs. W. B. Rulison, H. W. Byrnes, A. H. Brown, E. N. Crasto, L. F. Burgess, H. J. Hayter, J. Cowins, J. H. Egbert, E. H. Clement, C. C. Winans, W. J. Keatley, J. O. Foster (supply), F. H. Knight, P. S. Blight, S. T. Jackson, J. William Ryder, and Berryman H. McCoy.

The Rev. Berryman H. McCoy, the present pastor, was installed in April, 1912. The chapel was remodelled in the winter of 1909-10. The present membership of the church is 300, and of the Sunday-school, 450.

THE CHURCH OF THE SACRED HEART stands on the corner of Broad and Liberty streets, near the south-

BLOOMFIELD, OLD AND NEW 133

west corner of the Green, and its stately tower, 160 feet in height, is a conspicuous feature of the town. It is the loftiest landmark of this vicinity.

The Roman Catholics of Bloomfield originally formed part of the Immaculate Conception Parish of Montclair. In response to many petitions Bishop Corrigan, the late Archbishop of New York, at length ordered the formation of a new parish, and the Rev. Joseph M. Nardiello of Newark was appointed to take charge June 21, 1878. The Parish of the Sacred Heart was incorporated July 1, 1878, the lay trustees being Francis O'Brien and Edward Quinn. The latter dying seven months later, John McGrath was appointed in his place and served with Mr. O'Brien for many years.

Mass was at first celebrated in a hall in the Bloomfield Hotel: but the basement of a frame church on Bloomfield Avenue was completed and ready for occupancy by September 21st of the same year.

The first parochial school was erected June 4, 1882: the large primary school in July, 1902.

The corner-stone of the present church edifice facing the Park was laid on October 19, 1890, and it was completed just two years later, October 18, 1892. It is of mottled brick with terra-cotta and stone trimmings. The seating capacity is 800. The main altar, of Carrara marble, was the gift of the rector, and the memorial windows were presented by parishioners and friends. The consecration of the church by Archbishop, now Cardinal Satolli, took place with great ceremony on October 21, 1894.

The cemetery of Mt. Olivet was laid out in 1883, and its chapel erected in 1901. There is a Convent of Sisters and a Club-house for the use of the Young Men's

Catholic Lyceum connected with the church, besides the large parochial schools.

The Rev. Joseph M. Nardiello, the first rector of the new parish of Bloomfield, has continued in office ever since its organization, and to his energy its growth and prosperity are largely due. In 1902 he was made an Irremovable Rector. The silver jubilee of the organization of the church of the Sacred Heart, and of the pastorate of Rev. J. M. Nardiello, was celebrated in 1903. John J. Murray and Michael N. Higgins are the present lay trustees.

The present communicant membership of the church is about 2,000, and there are 586 in the Sunday-school.

THE GLEN RIDGE CONGREGATIONAL CHURCH, located on Ridgewood Avenue, corner of Clark Street, Glen Ridge, rightly has a place in this record, inasmuch as its organization antedates the separation of the two towns. A majority of the families of its original members came from the Westminster Church of Bloomfield, and the church is still included in the Bloomfield Evangelical Union.

Its origin was due to the need felt by some of the residents of Glen Ridge for church accommodations nearer than those of Bloomfield. Evening services were at first held in the Glen Ridge station of the Delaware, Lackawanna and Western Railroad by the courtesy of the company, beginning on January 22, 1888. Regular morning and evening services were opened on Sunday morning, March 11th, when the sermon was preached by Rev. Charles E. Knox, D.D., of Bloomfield. Its organization was effected on April 8, 1888, by a Congregational Council called for the purpose, forty-three persons uniting to form the Glen Ridge

Congregational Church. Ira Campbell, Marius G. Belloni and Arthur J. Lockwood were elected the first deacons of the new church. Rev. Frank J. Goodwin was called later to the pastorate, in which he was installed October 10, 1888, at a service held in the First Presbyterian Church of Bloomfield, Rev. R. S. Storrs, D.D., of Brooklyn, preaching the sermon. Members of the family of the late Rev. Joseph S. Gallagher, desiring to further the cause of Christ in the community, and to erect a suitable memorial to Mr. Gallagher, soon presented the beautifully situated piece of property upon which the grey stone church was erected. The donors were Mrs. Susan C. Gallagher, Miss Martha C. Gallagher, and Mr. and Mrs. Joseph D. Gallagher.

The first service was held in the new building on June 29, 1890; but the dedicatory service was not held until October 28, 1890. The edifice was re-built and greatly enlarged in 1902, and is now admirably adapted to serve the religious needs of the growing neighborhood to which it ministers.

Rev. Frank J. Goodwin, the first pastor, was succeeded after eleven years, in 1899, by Rev. Elliott Wilbur Brown, D.D., whose pastorate lasted ten years. Rev. Clarence Hall Wilson, D.D., the third and present pastor, was installed December 10, 1909.

The present membership of the church is 461, and of the Sunday-school, 296.

THE BROOKDALE BAPTIST CHURCH, situated in what was originally known as Stone House Plains, was first organized as a Methodist Church in 1873, and the present building was erected in 1874. For eighteen years the church was without a pastor. In 1893 Henry Hepburn bought the church, and under Rev. Charles C.

Cook, at that time pastor of the First Baptist Church of Bloomfield, it was organized as a mission of that church. The list of pastors has been as follows:

Rev. S. L. Harter 1894-1896
Rev. W. N. Hubbel 1897-1898
Rev. Henry Brittain 1899-1908

The Rev. Norman P. Smith, the present pastor, was installed in August, 1908. The present membership of the church is 62, and of the Sunday-school, 110.

ST. JOHN'S EVANGELICAL LUTHERAN CHURCH, situated on the corner of Liberty Street and Austin Place, was organized in 1896, and its present building was erected in 1901. The Rev. Mr. Ebendick, of Richfield, N. J., started the Lutheran services in Bloomfield in a hall in the Centre in 1895, preaching every Sunday afternoon. After the installation of Pastor Heyd the congregation erected a chapel in 1896 on the present location of the church. In 1901 the present church building was purchased from the Westminster Presbyterian Church and moved to Liberty Street and Austin Place, and the chapel was moved to the rear of the lot and joined to it, and is now used as a Sunday-school room. The church is now in the transition period from German to English. Most of the work in the Sunday-school is done in English, and regular English services are also held. The church and the Sunday-school are increasing steadily in membership through new families moving to Bloomfield from Greater New York and other nearby cities. A very active Ladies' Society, and a Young People's Society, are important factors in the growth of the church.

BLOOMFIELD, OLD AND NEW 137

The following has been the ministerial succession:

Rev. Albert Heyd 1896-1899
Rev. J. George F. Blaesi 1899-1900
Rev. J. Schulz 1900-1902
Rev. C. Ziegelbrier 1902-1903
Rev. H. A. Steininger 1903-1906
Rev. Fr. Noeldeke 1906-1908

Rev. C. H. Franke, the present pastor, was installed October 4, 1908. The present membership of the church is 275, and of the Sunday-school, 86. A German school is held every Saturday morning from 10 to 12 o'clock, in which German, Bible history and the catechism are taught.

ST. VALENTINE'S ROMAN CATHOLIC CHURCH, situated at Franklin Avenue, corner of Plane Street, ministers to the large Polish population at the north end of the town. The church was organized February 16, 1899, and the present building was erected in 1905. The corner-stone was laid on August 20th of that year by Rt. Rev. John J. O'Connor, Bishop of Newark, and on May 30, 1906, the new church was dedicated by the same bishop. The Rev. Constantine Zalinski, the first rector, was succeeded by Rev. John Adamowski, and Rev. Thadaeus Stankiewicz. The present rector is Rev. John A. Ivanow.

The present membership of the church is given as 1,010, and of the Sunday-school as 80. There is also a parochial school in connection with the church.

THE CHURCH OF THE ASCENSION, at the corner of Montgomery Street and Berkeley Avenue, of which the Rev. W. T. Lipton is rector, is the latest accession to the churches of Bloomfield. It was organized as a parochial mission of Christ Church, under the rectorship of the Rev. E. A. White, in the spring of 1901, and placed in charge of Colonel Wilson Vance, a lay reader. Services were held for a year and a half in a vacant store on the corner of Montgomery and Orchard streets.

In January, 1902, a lot on the corner of Montgomery and Berkeley avenues was purchased and paid for by the people associated with the chapel. The present church building was erected during that year, and the opening service was held on December 21st. In 1909 the status of the Church of the Ascension was changed from that of a parochial to that of an organized mission of the diocese. In January, 1910, the lot adjoining the church property was purchased and paid for.

Colonel Vance resigned in the autumn of 1902. He was succeeded by the Rev. L. R. Levering, who had charge until April, 1905. He was followed by the Rev. R. W. E. Merington, who resigned in June, 1906. The Rev. H. P. Scratchley then took charge. He resigned in December, 1908, and was succeeded by the Rev. W. T. Lipton, who became the first rector when the mission was organized and incorporated as a parish in April, 1911.

There are 110 communicants and 375 members. There are 12 teachers and 80 children in the Sunday-school.

The officers of the church are: Wardens, Arthur B. Albertis and J. R. Wilde; Vestrymen, S. A. Andrew, S. P. Bleecker, Henry C. De Witt, A. W. Graham, L. A. Kimball, S. P. Morton, Calvin Peck, A. H. Whitefield and F. L. H. Wood.

There is a Colored Baptist Church on Bloomfield Avenue, near the Centre. The members of the Hebrew

BLOOMFIELD, OLD AND NEW

Congregation meet in a building recently purchased on Bloomfield Avenue, Glen Ridge. No statistics of these are furnished.

THE GERMAN THEOLOGICAL SCHOOL OF NEWARK occupies the old academy building, which is situated in Bloomfield, on Franklin and Liberty streets, near the south end of the Green. The main recitation building was formerly the home of the Bloomfield Academy. This institution, now in its forty-third year, is under the care of the Presbyterian Church in the United States of America, and trains students for its ministry among our foreign-born population. Originally started for German students, its scope has been enlarged to include Italians, Hungarians, Ruthenians and a growing polyglot work among all nationalities in our country. Sixty students were enrolled last year. Rev. Charles E. Knox, D.D., resigned the pastorate of the First Presbyterian Church of Bloomfield in 1873, in order to accept the presidency of the institution, then in its infancy, and served it for twenty-seven years. It is intended to erect a fine new building, to be known as "Knox Hall," for recitation and chapel purposes in the near future. Rev. David R. Frazer, D.D., is president of the Board of Directors.

The Faculty is composed of Rev. Henry J. Weber, Ph.D., D.D., Professor of Theology and Church History; Rev. Carl T. Hock, Ph.D., D.D., Professor of Classics and Hebrew; Rev. Arnold W. Fismer, Ph.D., D.D., Professor of New Testament Exegesis and Ethics; Rev. Frederick W. Jackson, Ph.B., C.E., Professor of English Language and Literature; Rev. John Dikovics, Instructor in Hungarian; Rev. William A. Berger, M.A., Instructor in Mathematics.

MUNICIPAL DEVELOPMENT

By William P. Sutphen

The early settlers of Bloomfield who came from Newark were of English stock, while those who came from Bergen and settled in the northerly section were of Dutch descent. The tides met at Speertown, now Upper Montclair, and at Stone House Plains. From these came the founders of the old families of Bloomfield whose names are still familiar. Among the English were the Wards, the Davises, the Morrises, the Dodds and the Baldwins; and among the Dutch, the Cadmuses, the Cockefairs, the Siglers and the Van Giesens, not to mention others. These families developed large tracts of land, known as plantations. With the clearing of the land the fertile soil made the section a prosperous farming community; and with the increase in population there came the demand for industry.

The first mill of which we have any record is the old saw mill built on the Morris plantation, which bore on its corner stone the date "1702." The site of this mill was the corner of Bay Avenue and Morris Place. It served the people of the northern section for many generations, and its ruins remained until the year 1890, when they were torn down and removed. This old mill received its water from the Third River, which after furnishing power to saw the logs of the surrounding country, passed on just below the mill into Morris Pond, whose waters were drained many years ago. With the clearing of the forests more ponds were provided along the various streams to furnish power for the saw and

ALONG THE YANTECAW OR THIRD RIVER

grist mills, while bark obtained in the woods was used in the tanneries. To utilize the straw raised on the farms, paper mills were established; while other interests, taking advantage of the splendid water facilities, located in the same section. The Second and Third rivers, which pass through the town on their way to the Passaic River, furnished water power for the mills which gradually grew up upon their banks. The chief business center, however, developed upon the Passaic River, in that territory of Bloomfield Township known as Second River. With the transportation facilities afforded by a navigable stream it was natural that this site, later called Belleville, should develop as a business center.

Industrial development began shortly after the close of the War of 1812, and so rapid was its progress that by 1830 Bloomfield was known as a manufacturing village. At that time it contained six grist mills, two cotton manufactories, five saw mills, four copper rolling mills, three paper mills, one paint mill, two calico print works, three woolen manufactories, and several shoe factories, besides seventeen merchants. While the business development had been mainly along the bank of the Passaic River, there had also been considerable growth near the mountains along the smaller streams. Convenient means of travel were afforded early in the last century by the building of turnpikes, conducted as toll roads, reaching to Newark and as far west as Pompton, while added impetus was given to industrial development in 1831 when the Morris Canal was built through the township. This offered another means of transit for passengers as well as for freight, and was of particular benefit to the industries in the transportation of crude material, and of the finished product, forwarded to the Newark and New York markets. On this waterway a packet boat, launched in 1832, ran for several years between Newark and Paterson, stopping at Bloomfield. This new means of transportation added greatly to the advantages of the central section of the town for the development of manufactories.

In 1839 the Second River section of the township, bordering on the Passaic River, which had long since become known as Belleville, was set off as a separate municipality. This partition not only reduced the importance of Bloomfield as a commercial center, but also reduced the population about one-half. According to the census of 1840, the year after the separation, the population of Belleville was 2,466, while that of Bloomfield was 2,528. Notwithstanding this loss, Bloomfield contained in that year three paper, one cotton and two woolen factories, one dyeing and printing establishment, one fulling mill, one copper rolling mill, two grist mills, two saw mills, and one button factory. These plants, however, were small compared with those in the Belleville section, for it was but natural that those planning large manufacturing establishments should locate upon tide water, where every facility for water transportation could be secured. At this time the capital employed in manufacturing in Belleville was $479,000, while that invested in the industries remaining in Bloomfield was only $111,000.

In 1856, through the efforts of enterprising Bloomfielders, the Newark and Bloomfield Railroad was completed. This road, which was operated as a branch of the Morris and Essex, added greatly to the development of the town; for while it enabled the local manufacturer to transport his finished product to the metropolitan market, it also afforded an opportunity for the business man of the city to make his home in the country, where his family could enjoy the delights of field and wood, avoiding the noise and dust of the city. With these added facilities there began the growth of the commuting element, which has become such a large proportion of the present population. The delightful location of Bloomfield, with its wide streets, magnificent elms, and comfortable old homesteads, proved attractive to business men seeking a country home, near enough to the city for them to attend business each day without spending too much time in travel.

The construction of the New York and Greenwood Lake Railroad in 1872 opened up another section of the town, and afforded increased facilities for transportation and travel.

Shortly after the close of the Civil War there began increased activity in Bloomfield real estate; several ventures were undertaken in this line, one of the largest by Robert Peele, who developed a large section in the western part of the township. With increased demand for building lots, there naturally developed a desire for street improvements, for up to this time the streets were simply graded, no pavements being laid either on the sidewalks or the roadways. With the increased demand the improvements gradually came. First, the stone sidewalk, followed by gas street lamps, and then a few of the streets were macadamized. The people of Bloomfield, however, were rather conservative about running into debt for improvements, as they had been in 1868, when on the question of bonding for the Greenwood Lake Railway, those in the northern end of the township, known as Montclair, wishing the improvement, withdrew and set up a government of their own. While this spirit of conservatism has to some extent held back needed improvements, it has prevented any rash step through all the years of the town's history.

In early years industrial development came as a result of abundant water power, while in recent years transportation facilities have been mainly responsible for such growth. In addition to the two railways mentioned, a branch of the Greenwood Lake Railroad, running to Orange, traverses the southern section of the town. With three railroad lines and the Morris Canal, the facilities for bringing fuel and raw products within easy reach, and even to the doors of the manufactories, have been of tremendous advantage to enterprising business men, with the result that while capital invested in manufacturing establishments in the year 1840, just after Belleville separated from the township, was $111,000, it is now approximately $8,000,000.

One of the old establishments, which is still in operation, is the woolen mill started by David Oakes in the year 1830. This great plant has been kept in the family, and the business is now conducted under the firm name of Thomas Oakes and Company. These mills are well known throughout the country through the established reputation of their product. They now employ about 450 people.

The modern industrial growth has occurred during the last twenty years. In 1890 the Consolidated Safety Pin Company moved to Bloomfield, establishing its large industry along Tony's Brook, near the Lackawanna Railroad. While manufacturing establishments may be found in various parts of the town, the principal in-

BLOOMFIELD, OLD AND NEW 145

dustrial section has developed near the junction of the Orange Branch of the Greenwood Lake Railroad, and the Newark and Bloomfield Branch of the Lackawanna Railroad. During the last two decades the following large establishments have located in Bloomfield: The Sprague Electric Elevator Company, now a branch of the General Electric Company, the Diamond Mills Paper Company, the H. B. Wiggins Sons Company, manufacturers of wall coverings, the Empire Cream Separator Company, the Combination Rubber Manufacturing Company, Scott and Bowne, manufacturers of Scott's Emulsion, and the Westinghouse Lamp Company, producing incandescent lamps. The last mentioned industry is the largest in the town, and employs about 1,500 hands. This industry was removed to Bloomfield in 1907. There are now nearly fifty manufacturing establishments in the community, of a widely diversified character, which insures permanent employment to a large proportion of the citizens of the town, while hundreds of employees in these industries come from the neighboring municipalities. The labor is mainly skilled and largely native born.

The increase in population has been steady, and at certain periods rapid, as the following table of United States Census figures will show:

1820	3,085	1870	4,580
1830	4,309	1880	5,748
1840	2,528	1890	7,708
1850	3,385	1900	9,668
1860	4,790	1910	15,070

The decrease in population noted in the figures for 1840 and 1870 is due to the separation of Belleville in 1839 and Montclair in 1868.

In 1871 the Bloomfield Savings Institution was founded, the first president being Warren S. Baldwin. This oldest of the financial institutions has aided greatly in the development of the town by promoting thrift among its inhabitants. Beginning business on May 9, 1871, it has by conservative management steadily grown until on January 1, 1912, with nearly 4,000 depositors, its deposits amounted to $1,185,000, and its surplus was $115,000. The first meeting of the board of managers was held at the residence of the founder, Zophar B. Dodd, at the northeastern corner of Liberty and State streets. The business was carried on in the basement of the Dodd house until 1889, when the office was removed to the Hill Building at Bloomfield Center. Succeeding Mr. Baldwin, the following gentlemen have served as presidents of this institution: Israel C. Ward, 1874; Jonathan W. Potter, 1886; William H. White, 1889; and Theodore H. Ward since 1904. The interest paid on deposits has ranged from 7 per cent. from 1871-75, to 3 per cent. from 1885-94. Since 1910 4 per cent. has been paid on all amounts. In 1910 the Savings Institution erected on Broad Street, at Bloomfield Center, a building to be devoted entirely to the business of the bank. This building with a monumental front is a very attractive feature of the town.

With the growth of the population, and the increase in business, the need of a banking institution with larger powers was realized, and to provide this want the Bloomfield National Bank was organized on May 18, 1889, with the following directors: Thomas Oakes, G. Lee Stout, Halsey M. Barrett, James C. Beach, A. G. Darwin, Edward G. Ward, Henry K. Benson,

Willard Richards, Henry P. Dodd, William Colfax, John P. Scherff, Edmund H. Davey, Robert S. Rudd, Polyhemus Lyon, and William A. Baldwin. The bank opened for business on July 1, 1889, with the following officers: President, Thomas Oakes; Vice-President, William A. Baldwin; Cashier, Lewis K. Dodd. These officials have continued to direct the affairs of the institution up to the present time. The first office of the bank was at No. 1 Broad Street. In 1901 the bank removed to its present building at the corner of Broad Street and Bloomfield Avenue, where Martin's grocery store had been located for many years. This handsome bank building was the first pretentious structure erected at Bloomfield Center. The original capital of the National Bank was $50,000, which has recently been increased to $100,000. The institution which was founded to provide banking facilities for the community has proved to be a profitable investment for its founders. The growth in business has been steady, and on January 1, 1912, its deposits amounted to $1,466,000; while the surplus and undivided profits were $48,000.

The Bloomfield Trust Company is the most recent banking institution established in the town, having been organized in 1902, with a capital of $100,000 and a surplus of $20,000. The original directors were John Sherman, Joseph H. Dodd, William R. Broughton, William H. White, Edwin M. Ward, Edward Oakes, Robert M. Boyd, Jr., N. Harvey Dodd, John M. Van Winkle, James N. Jarvie, W. W. Snow, A. R. Brewer, and Allison Dodd.

Dr. William H. White was elected president, and Joseph H. Dodd, secretary. The growth of the trust company has been very rapid, the deposits on January

1, 1912, amounting to $1,560,000, while the surplus and undivided profits amounted to $141,000, the original surplus of $20,000 having been returned to the stockholders. Their new building at the corner of Bloomfield and Glenwood avenues at Bloomfield Center is a substantial fire-proof office building of attractive exterior, containing fully equipped offices both for the trust company and for the use of tenants. In March, 1912, they moved from their original location at No. 1 Broad Street to their new building across the square.

Few municipalities of the size of Bloomfield have three bank buildings equal to those at Bloomfield Center, and the banking facilities afforded the people of the town by these institutions are all that are needed even for a community with such varied and extensive interests as are found in modern Bloomfield.

This town is notably a community of homes. While there are not many large estates, the number of citizens who own their own homes is unusually large. This is due in large measure to the encouragement and support offered by building and loan associations, which have played an important part in the development of the town. The Essex County Building and Loan Association is the oldest of these, having been organized October 18, 1885. This association is one of the largest and most prosperous in the State of New Jersey, and is recognized as a model institution of its kind. By its last report it showed assets amounting to $900,000, while during its history over $5,500,000 of savings have been disbursed, a large part of which was used to acquire homes. The Bloomfield Building and Loan Association, while smaller, is a prosperous organization of some years standing; while the Merchants and Me-

BLOOMFIELD, OLD AND NEW 149

chanics, and the Prospect-Watsessing Building and Loan Association have recently been organized. All of these institutions are managed by local men who have given freely of their time and thought, the results of which have proved of great benefit, particularly to the man of small means who, without the assistance secured through such resources, would be unable to raise the necessary funds to build a home for his family.

In the winter of 1882-3 two disastrous fires occurred near the center of the town, one destroying Archdeacons' Hotel, while the other resulted in the loss of a large shop and several dwellings, notwithstanding the determined efforts of volunteers to prevent the spread of the flames. These heavy losses brought sharply to the attention of the citizens the absolute necessity for fire-fighting apparatus to prevent the repetition of such destructive fires. On June 27, 1883, Essex Hook and Ladder Company No. 1 was organized, and a truck was purchased with volunteer subscriptions. This organization received the enthusiastic support of the citizens of the entire community, and the young men heartily volunteered to perform fire duty. Not only did they render good service in this connection, but the truck house became a social center where the men might spend their evenings. On November 2, 1883, Bloomfield Hose Company No. 1 was organized, and the township provided it with a jumper and hose. In September, the following year, it changed its name to the Phœnix Hose Company No. 1, and purchased a handsome hose carriage.

Not until 1883 were water mains laid in the streets of the town. The first contract, made with the Orange Water Company, provided for ten miles of mains and ninety-six fire hydrants. The first chief of the fire department was Andrew J. Marsh, since then the office has been held by T. Howell Johnson, William U. Oakes, Edgar D. Ackerman, B. F. Higgins, and James Y. Nicoll. In 1885 Active Hose Company No. 2 was organized in the southern end of the town, and Excelsior Hose Company was organized and located in Upper Broad Street, at the corner of James. The need of protection in the southeastern section caused the formation, in 1904, of Montgomery Hose Company No. 4 and Brookdale Hose Company No. 5 was organized in 1911.

An electric fire alarm system throughout the town permits of a quick call in time of need. The fire department is still volunteer and has a splendid record, of which the entire town is proud. On July 8, 1908, the twenty-fifth anniversary of the organization of the department was celebrated, and was a gala day in the old town. Hundreds of visiting firemen attended the ceremonies which appropriately marked the occasion.

The only public municipal buildings owned by the town are the fire houses, consisting of the double truck and hose house on Bloomfield Avenue, near the Center, and the houses occupied by Active, Excelsior and Montgomery hose companies. Early in 1912 the efficiency of the department was increased by the purchase of a combination chemical wagon.

As has been stated, the water system of the town was owned by the Orange Water Company. This company supplied water to the municipality and to the citizens for many years. In the year 1903 the question of municipal ownership was agitated. The water company asked $220,000 for its mains in the streets. This amount was reduced to $150,000 by the company, but the proposition was rejected by the voters at an election. At a public meeting of the citizens the Council was asked to offer the water company $90,000 for their plant. This was done, and the offer was accepted. Bloomfield thereupon embarked upon the unknown sea of municipal ownership with many misgivings on the part of the conservative element of the community. As the town had no source of supply, it was necessary to make a contract for its requirements. After a thorough investigation, in which the Board of Trade and Civic Union co-operated, a contract was entered into with the Montclair Water Company, a subsidiary of the East Jersey Water Company, by which the town secured a long term contract for filtered water from the Upper Passaic, at $65 per million gallons. The result has been that municipal ownership, as carried on in Bloomfield, has proved of immense advantage to the town. Not only have the rates to the consumers been materially reduced since the acquisition of the plant, but the municipality makes no provision in its tax budget for water consumed, and the water department is making a net profit of more than $15,000 per year. This result has been secured only by the conducting of the department on a strictly business basis.

A system of sewers was constructed in the year 1898, while macadamized road construction on a large scale was undertaken the following year. These improvements mark the beginning of a progressive policy in the town which has been generally supported by the people in succeeding years.

Many fraternities have established lodges in the town, some of them reaching back to the first quarter of the last century. These orders have had a large influence in shaping the political and social life of the community. Outside of societies connected with the churches the following are the most important fraternal and patriotic orders:

>Grand Army of the Republic,
>Sons of Veterans,
>Ancient Order of Hibernians,
>Benevolent and Protective Order of Elks,
>Daughters of Liberty,
>Free and Accepted Masons,
>Improved Order of Heptasophs,
>Independent Order of Foresters,
>Independent Order of Odd Fellows,
>Junior Order United American Mechanics,
>Knights of Columbus,
>Knights of Honor,
>Knights of the Maccabees,
>Knights of Pythias,
>K. U. V. Freundschaft Bund,
>Loyal Association,
>Modern Woodmen of America,
>Royal Arcanum,
>Brotherhood of America.

The following are the names of the several Polish organizations, as furnished by their representatives: The Saint Valentine Polish Association, The Saint Rosary Men's Social Society, The Poniotawski Social Club, The Polish Fife and Drum Corps, The Sobieski Organization, and the Falkon Club.

Among the earlier associations which have had an important influence in the development of Bloomfield was the Eucleian Society of young men, organized in 1865, formed for "the improvement in mental culture of its members and the cultivation of a literary taste in our village." The meetings were held in Eucleian Hall, over Horace Pierson's store, at the northeast corner of Glenwood and Washington avenues at the Center, and the society frequently provided lecture courses in which noted public speakers appeared. Growing out of this society there developed the Bloomfield Library Association, which planned the building of a large public hall, and the foundation of a public library. The hall was built in 1874, and was used for many years for public gatherings of all kinds, but unfortunately, the enterprise was not a success financially, and the library was never secured. A free public library was organized in the Watsessing section of the town in 1886 and proved of value to that part of the community for some years. In 1902, James N. Jarvie erected to the memory of his parents, William J. and Mary N. Jarvie, a parish house for the Westminster Presbyterian Church, including in the architectural scheme a public library. An endowment of $50,000 was given to insure an adequate sum for the securing of new books and periodicals from year to year. The library started with 5,200 volumes and now contains about 15,000. The reading-rooms are entirely free, and, for $1 a year any resident of Bloomfield or vicinity may draw books from the circulating department. The trustees of Westminster Church are *ex-officio* trustees of the Jarvie Memorial Library. The library, however, is conducted strictly as a public library. A large and rapidly growing circulation demonstrates its value to the community.

During the closing years of the last century a vocal organization known as the Madrigal Society developed the musical taste of the community, giving two concerts each year. For fifteen years the annual course of literary and musical entertainments under the auspices of the Guild of the First Presbyterian Church has been an important feature of the life of the community. In 1902 the need of united action on the part of those citizens desiring the proper development of the town was realized, and to secure co-operation a Board of Trade was organized on February 5th. Its first regular meeting was held on March 19th of that year, and the following officers elected: Thomas McGowan, president; Joseph F. Vogelius, vice-president; Peter J. Quinn, secretary; and Charles R. Underwood, treasurer. Those who have held the position of president following Mr. McGowan have been William P. Sutphen, William Biggart, Frederic M. Davis, and Charles A. Hungerford. This organization has had a large influence in the development of the town. Beginning with 34, it now has on its roll about 400 members. Not only has it exerted its influence in matters governmental, but it has taken up all lines of civic development. In this organization originated the idea of observing the present centennial, and the report of its committee on the centennial will be found in an appendix. Two features which were introduced early in its history were the annual dinner and the Fourth of July celebration. The first dinner was held on April 16, 1903, at which eighty-six persons were present. This affair has become an important event in the town, prominent speakers being secured to address the gathering, which has grown so large that it is difficult to find a hall sufficiently large to accommodate those desiring to attend. Probably the most popular project undertaken by the board was the celebration of Independence Day, which was first undertaken with many misgivings in 1905, with a parade and an oration in the morning, athletic events in the afternoon, and fireworks in the evening. The undertaking was so successful from the first that it has become the most popular celebration of the year, and not only has it been enjoyed by our own citizens, but thousands have come from surrounding communities to share in the festivities. The expense of the celebration has been met by popular subscription, the amount in recent years exceeding $1,000.

At the time of the San Francisco disaster in 1906, a committee was appointed to receive donations for the relief of the Pacific Coast sufferers, with the result that $2,316 was raised in a few days for this purpose. As has been previously mentioned, a special committee of the Board of Trade was of material assistance to the town authorities in making a favorable contract in 1905 for a supply of water.

While Bloomfield has been most fortunate in having as one of its chief attractions a park equal to the village greens of New England towns, it was felt by the members of the Board of Trade that this community should receive some share of the funds expended by Essex County, in the development of a park system which has few equals. Accordingly, that organization appointed a park committee on June 8, 1905, consisting of William R. Broughton, Charles R. Underwood, D. G. Garrabrant, Edward G. Ward and Samuel Ellor; Allison Dodd was added to the committee later. Bloomfield being one of the smaller municipalities of the county, the possibility of securing county funds for park purposes seemed very doubtful, and even those who were in a position to assist in the endeavor were very pessimistic as to the outcome. In the fall of that year

Mr. Underwood, a member of the committee, was elected a member of the House of Assembly. A bill was introduced authorizing the expenditure of additional park funds in Essex County. Here was Bloomfield's opportunity, and Mr. Underwood took full advantage of it. He insisted that if the bill was to be passed it should provide funds to be expended in Bloomfield. After much effort he was successful in reaching an understanding with his colleagues in the Assembly, and a bill appropriating $300,000 became a law. It then became necessary to have the Essex County Park Commission expend the funds authorized in the municipalities for which they were intended. This was no easy task, for some citizens of Newark who were interested in a park scheme toward which part of the funds covered by the appropriation were to go, insisted that they should receive that portion which had been intended for Bloomfield. Mr. Underwood appeared before the Commission, and with the support of his colleagues in the Legislature, convinced them that Bloomfield was entitled to those funds which had been originally provided for in the Act. As a result, $60,000 was expended by the Park Commission in securing low lands lying west of the Lackawanna Railroad, between the Bloomfield and Watsessing stations. While property in other sections of the town might have been secured for park purposes at a lower figure, it was realized by the municipal authorities and the Board of Trade Committee that unless this land, which lay at the approach to the town, was developed as a park, it would build up most unattractively, and become a real detriment, as those visiting the town would receive in that event most unfavorable impressions. Not only was this an important reason for

BLOOMFIELD, OLD AND NEW 157

the location of the park in the section named, but this land was adjacent to the section where the population was most congested. These two considerations determined the County Park Commission to expend the money in the purchase of the property recommended. The park committee of the Board of Trade was instrumental in securing the land at most reasonable figures. Up to the year 1910 over $160,000 was appropriated by the county for the purchase and improvement of land in Bloomfield for park purposes. Altogether, about thirty-five acres of land west of the Lackawanna Railroad was secured by the Park Commission. The same conditions prevailed regarding the low land lying east of the Lackawanna Railroad, and in order to secure a satisfactory improvement, it was realized that the land on the east should be improved as well as that on the west of the railroad. The Park Commission at first refused to expend any funds on the easterly side. It was then realized that the municipal authorities would have to do their share in the work in order to secure the desired improvement. The sum of $25,000 was appropriated by the town. As the plans developed, it was found necessary to increase this amount to about $52,000, and the County Park Commission was persuaded to expend $25,000 in this section, the result being that about twenty-five acres were secured for a playground, bounded by the Lackawanna Railroad and Bloomfield Avenue, Conger Street and Roosevelt Avenue, the last being a new street laid out in 1909 as the southern boundary of the Park. The land to which the town took title was turned over to the care, custody and control of the Essex County Park Commission for development and maintenance, in order that the town might not be put to this expense. Large public improvements are secured slowly, and frequently with great difficulty, and while the property has been secured, the development has not yet been undertaken. It is confidently expected that the Commission will shortly improve the land and that before long it will be made a beautiful park and playground for the delight, not only of our citizens, but of all those who travel through our town by the Lackawanna Railroad. The chief credit for securing this most valuable asset to the town of Bloomfield is due the park committee of the Board of Trade and particularly Charles R. Underwood and Allison Dodd.

The amount of bonded indebtedness for the Bloomfield parks was made $60,000 to purchase the property for the playground and to secure and improve land in the triangular plot in the Second Ward, bounded by Broad Street, Bay Avenue, and Morris Place. A number of owners of lots in this plot donated their property for park purposes, but some of it had to be acquired by purchase. In securing this property the Board of Trade's park committee was also of great assistance to the town authorities.

The approach to the Town of Bloomfield by the Lackawanna Railroad Company as far back as the "eighties" had been a source of annoyance to those citizens of the town who desired that newcomers might receive pleasing first impressions, for the railroad station at Glenwood Avenue had become an eyesore, and its surroundings were not at all attractive. A movement was started at that time by the Rev. Samuel W. Duffield, pastor of Westminster Presbyterian Church, and a progressive citizen, to secure the construction of a new station and the improvement of surrounding conditions; but on account of the interests of some of the property owners in the neighborhood, he was unable to secure the desired improvements. The matter was allowed to drift along for many years. From time to time there were rumors that the Lackawanna Company were to improve their approach, but nothing developed until about the year 1902, when the railroad company made a proposal to the town officials looking to the elevation of the tracks at Glenwood Avenue and Washington Street, and the erection of a new station at that point, the town to assume $40,000 of the cost of the change. The town authorities did not see their way clear to assume this expense, and the matter was dropped. It was revived by the Board of Trade in 1903, but the Lackawanna Railroad was not in a position to undertake the work at that time, on account of the improvements which they were carrying out through the city of Newark. Early in the year 1907 the subject was taken up in earnest, and negotiations undertaken to secure the abolition of the grade crossings at Glenwood Avenue and Washington Street, and the erection of a new station at Bloomfield proper. These negotiations had proceeded to a point where the town authorities considered it proper to hold a public hearing, when the citizens of the southern section of the town made urgent demand upon the Town Council that the Railroad Company eliminate the grade crossings in that section of the town at the same time that the other work should be undertaken, or at least give some guarantee that they should be eliminated within a reasonable time. The principal difficulties in the way, according to the railroad company, were the Erie Railroad crossing, and the refusal of the city of East Orange to enter into any agreement for a change of grade in its streets. After long delay, the Lackawanna and the Erie Railroad came to an understanding regarding the crossing at Watsessing, and a temporary grade was planned in East Orange which made it unnecessary to change the grade of the only street in that municipality on the Bloomfield division. Even after these obstacles had been overcome, the question of industrial switches, property damage, the location of stations and other details which affected many interests, made the negotiations of a contract with the railroad company extremely difficult. To assist in the negotiations, the Town Council employed a consulting engineer and a consulting architect who, with the town attorneys holding office during this period, Charles F. Kocher and A. B. Van Liew, together with the town engineer, Ernest Baechlin, worked out with the Town Council the solution of the various problems which arose as the negotiations progressed. Not only was there difficulty in the negotiation, but there was much opposition for various reasons to the improvement. After years of effort, an agreement, negotiated by Mr. Van Liew, was entered into with the Lackawanna Railroad Company on July 12, 1910, by which six grade crossings were to be eliminated, new stations erected on Lackawanna Place (a new street to be laid out on the east side of the railroad between Washington Street and Glenwood Avenue), and at Watsessing Avenue. The estimated cost to the railroad company for this work was $750,000, while the estimated expense to the town was figured at about $20,000. After many years the improvements which had been desired by the progressive citizens of Bloomfield were finally realized, the work being commenced in August, 1910, and completed in 1912.

With railroad changes and improvements, and the development of parks on either side of the track, the approach to the town of Bloomfield, when finally completed, will be so altered that it will be difficult to remember the miserable conditions which surrounded our railroad stations before the changes were undertaken; and it is impossible to estimate the value which these improved conditions will be to the municipality in making attractive the approach to the town, which approach is so important a feature of every community.

Not only have the men of the community been busy in securing betterments. In May, 1907, the women, wishing to have some part in town progress, organized a Town Improvement Association, which has been helpful in stimulating the activity of town officials along right lines, and in aiding the school children to an appreciation of their part in making the town a better place to live in.

Bloomfield has made great strides in the last few years, and the outlook for the old town is most promising. The effect of the development which has taken place will not be temporary, but is bound to continue for many years to come.

THE ANNALS OF STONE HOUSE PLAINS
OR
BROOKDALE

By James E. Brooks

The northern portion of the Town of Bloomfield, New Jersey, has been known as "Brookdale" since 1873, when the post-office was located there. The old name, "Stone House Plains," was too long, and "Brookdale" was adopted at a meeting of citizens held at the time. It is said that the name was suggested by a man who had been in Brookdale, Kansas.

The township of Newark, settled in 1666 by a company of English colonists from Connecticut, was bounded on the north by a line running northwest from the mouth of the Yantecaw or Third River. This line is now the boundary between Essex and Passaic counties.

A few years after the settlement of Newark, a company of Dutchmen secured a deed from the Indians, and a patent from the proprietors, for a large tract of land adjoining the township of Newark on the north. This was called Acquackanonk, and included the present township of Acquackanonk, the city of Passaic, and a part of the city of Paterson, all now in Passaic County.

As the settlers spread over the two townships the Dutch appear to have moved more rapidly than the English, for they pushed their settlements southward until a wide strip across the northern part of the Newark township was made up of Dutch communities.

These communities were known as "Second River," now Belleville; "Third River," now Nutley; "Stonehouse Plain," now Brookdale; and "Speer Town," now Upper Montclair.

Of these, Brookdale has changed the least; the land is still farmed by the families who originally settled there two hundred years ago, and the products of the soil are still taken to market in the farmers' wagons.

These Dutch communities, although within the political bounds of Newark until 1812, and Bloomfield after that, always maintained their social and religious allegiances among themselves, or to their Dutch neighbors to the north, rather than to their English neighbors to the south.

Now and then individuals would cross the boundary between English and Dutch, as when Alexander Cockefair married Phoebe Morris about 1750; or when Ephraim Morris married Catherine Cockefair in 1798. Occasionally outsiders entered and cast their lot with the people of Stone House Plains, as when Starr Parsons, the young Connecticut teacher, married Betsy Speer, and Joshua C. Brokaw, another teacher, from New York, married Maria Sigler; but these were the exceptions.

The Acquackanonk Purchase

The Indians had a village at the site of the present city of Passaic, it was located there because of the good fishing at the head of tide water on the Passaic River. They also gathered in large numbers about the time of our Thanksgiving Day for an annual feast, and a series of games and contests at the mouth of Third River. The name Yantecaw is a corruption of two Indian words meaning a ceremonial dance.

The aborigines never had any idea of the right of property in land. Such a thing is unknown to primitive races. But the Indians were willing enough to accept various trifles in the way of knives, beads, blankets and rum, and to sign a deed relinquishing their rights to the land; and they would sometimes sell the same land to other purchasers who might be supplied with other trinkets. The Indians were generally surprised to find that they had deeded away a much larger tract than they had intended. These facts led to differences between the white purchasers themselves, and between the white purchasers and the Indians. The proprietors of East Jersey made grants of land to settlers, but left it to the settlers themselves to make their own terms with the Indians. Sometimes purchasers of Indian lands failed to obtain title from the proprietors, and in some cases this led to serious collisions with the authorities. Several members of the Van Giesen family of Stone House Plains in 1746 got into difficulties in this way over the "Van Giesen Purchase," an account of which may be found in the "New Jersey Archives."

Christopher Hooglandt, a merchant of New York, on the recommendation of Jacob Stoffelson, a man well acquainted with the Indians, secured a grant from Sir George Carteret, the governor, for a small tract of land lying within the limits of the present city of Passaic. This was in 1678. He sold this to Hartman Michaelson in 1680. Hartman Michaelsen then secured from the Indians, Captahen, sachem and chief, and the minor sachems, a deed for the tract of land now consisting of the city of Passaic, part of Paterson, and all the present township of Acquackanonk. The consideration was a lot of coats, blankets, kettles, powder and other goods. This enterprising promoter then organized a company, and obtained from the proprietors of East Jersey, on March 30, 1684, a patent for this land sold to him by the Indians. The fourteen men in this company were:

Hans Diedricks,
Garret Garretsen,
Walling Jacobse,
Elias Michaelsen,
Hartman Michaelsen,
Cornelius Michaelsen,
Johannis Michaelsen,
Adrian Post,
Urian Thomassen,
Cornelius Roelfsen,
Symon Jacobse,
John Hendrick Spier,
Cornelius Lubers,
Abraham Bookey.

This list of names offers a good opportunity for explaining a Dutch custom. The family name of the four brothers, Elias, Cornelius, Hartman and Johannis, was not Michaelsen, it was Vreeland. The word Michaelsen meant their father's first, or Christian, name was Michael. Family names were not in general use among the Dutch at that time of the settlement of New Jersey. People adopted family names from many sources, such as the place where they lived, their trade, or some personal peculiarity. The result was that sometimes different branches of the same family adopted different names.

Of the fourteen associates in the Acquackanonk patent, Hans Diedricks never settled on the new possessions, and Abraham Bookey stayed but a short time.

Some of Garret Garretsen's descendants took the family name of Van Wagener, and some the name of Garrison. In the same way, some of Cornelius Lubers descendants are Westervelts, and some Van Blarcoms. Walling and Symon Jacobs were the ancestors of the Van Winkle family; Urian Thomassen of the Van Riper family; and Cornelius Roelfsen of the Van Houten family. But of all the fourteen the descendants of John Hendrick Spier are the most numerous. Speertown, now Upper Montclair, was but one of their strongholds. The spelling of names is something wonderful, if not awful. William Nelson, of Paterson, the historian, has found Acquackanonk spelled more than thirty different ways. The present investigation has found the family name of Cockefair with the following variations in spelling: Cokcover, Kockes, Cockhvier, Cockcoever, Coqueuert, Coquer, Cokever, Cokiver, Cokefair, Kokhefeer, Cockiefeer, Kockyser, Kockyefeer, Cokkifer, Cottiefer, Cokefer, Coccifer, Coufer, Cockafair, Cockafer, Cockefer, Kocjefer, Cockkifer, Cokifer, Cockifair, Cockifer and Cocifer. It is the family tradition that the proper spelling is Coquefaire. Not satisfied with such a liberal assortment of spellings, a few years ago one member of the family changed his name to Coxford.

The Settlement at Second River

Within a year or two after the first settlement of Acquackanonk, several Dutchmen purchased from members of the Newark company tracts of land within the present limits of Belleville and Nutley. The resulting settlements were known as Second River and Third River. Bastien Van Giesen, Tunis Jansen Pier, Claes Hendrickson and Hans Hendrickson Spier were among the number.

Hans Hendrickson Spier, a brother of John Hendrick Spier of Acquackanonk, was married at the Dutch Church in New York to Trijntie Pieters, on the first day of August, 1683. Hans and Trijntie probably settled at Second River soon after this, for their son

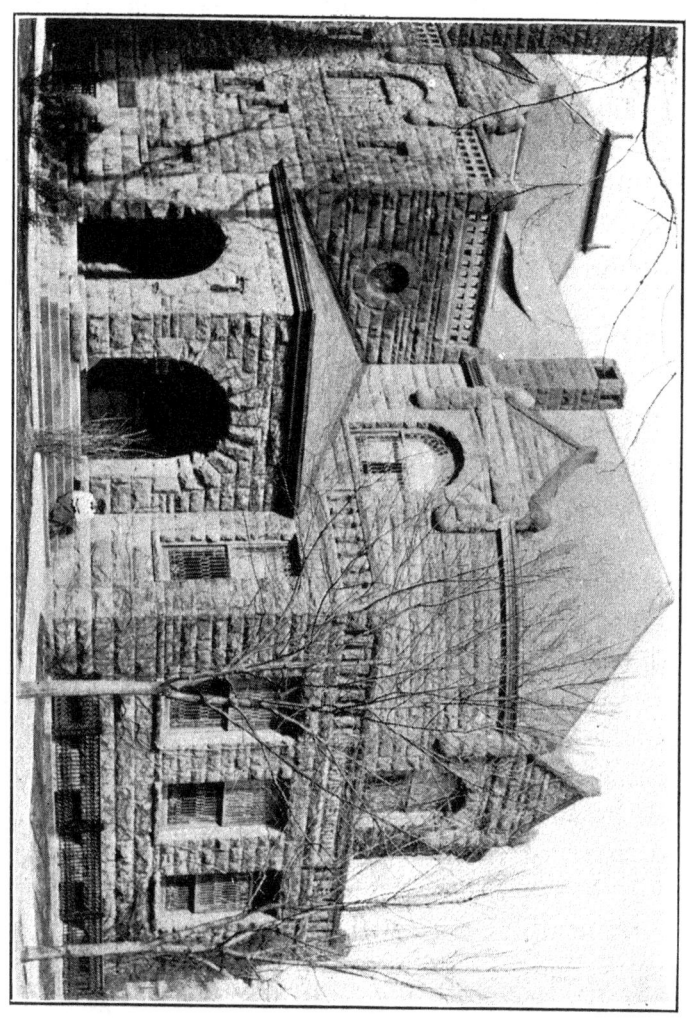

JARVIE MEMORIAL LIBRARY

Hendrick, baptized in October, 1685, was born there When Hendrick grew up and was married to Rachel Teunese Pier in 1708, at the Hackensack Church, the record stated that both he and his bride had been born and were living in the jurisdiction of Newark. Additional evidence is shown by a deed for sixty acres of land sold by Samuel Ward of Newark to Tunis Johnson Pier, July 15, 1685. This tract was bounded as follows: N. Hans Hendrickson Spier, E. Passaic River S. Second River. The west, not mentioned, was probably unsurveyed land.

The Old Stone House

The earliest owners of land in Brookdale were members of the Newark company who lived around the Newark green and held these outlying lots and tracts for future use; most of which were sold later to Dutch settlers. The eastern portion of the Jackson farm on Third River, purchased in 1911 by the Country Club of Glen Ridge, was, in 1696, part of a tract belonging to Samuel Plum. North of Samuel Plum was land of Robert Young, and further north Eliphalet Johnston, Daniel Dode and Samuel Kitchell; to the west of Eliphalet Johnston, the land of Samuel Huntington. Mention of the deeds and patents for these tracts is in Vol. XXI, N. J. Archives. These deeds and patents mention Stonehouse Brook as early as 1696, and Stonehouse Plain in 1697.

The use of the name Stonehouse as early as 1696 would indicate that some one had built a stone house along the little brook that bears that name, some time before, and there is much evidence to indicate that such was the case. There is a story, however, to the effect that the so-called "stone house" was not a human habitation but an overhanging ledge of rock, used as shelter by early travellers both white and Indian. The location of this "house" was in the old quarry north of the Stone House Plains Dutch Church, and on the opposite side of Bellevue Avenue. It was from this quarry that the stone was taken to build the church and the various stone houses in the neighborhood.

On the other hand there are those who believe that the "stone house" was not only built by human hands before 1696, but that it is still standing and in use. The house referred to stands near the south bank of Stone House Brook just across the Montclair boundary line and north of Bellevue Avenue. It is but a few hundred feet from the old quarry. The old house faces the east, and an examination shows that the southern end is much older than the larger portion to the north. The original house was square, twenty-one and a half feet each way, with one story and attic. Two courses of stone seem to have been added at some time to increase the height of the walls. There is a Dutch oven extending out beyond the south gable wall.

It is thought that the old stone house was built by Abraham Van Giesen, a brother of Bastien of Second River, about 1691, but the fact has not been proved. Through the courtesy of the Fidelity Trust Company the ownership of the house was traced back to 1818, and from the surrogate's office it was learned that the house belonged to Garret Van Wagener, whose will was proved in 1804. Further investigation indicates that Garret's parents were Hendrick Van Wagener and Anna Van Winkel, that he was born January 14, 1753, and married Jane Van Winkel. Nothing has been found that would show how the house came into his possession.

THE "STONE HOUSE" OF THE "PLAINS"

THE VAN GIESEN FAMILY

Reynier Bastiensen Van Giesen lived at Flatbush, Long Island, where, in June, 1661, he entered into an agreement with the magistrates, and the consistory of the Reformed Dutch Church of that place, to teach school, perform the duties of court messenger, ring the bell, keep the church in order, perform the duties of precentor, attend to the burial of the dead, and to all that was necessary and proper in the premises, for an annual salary of two hundred florins, exclusive of perquisites. In January, 1663, he sold his house and lot in Flatbush to Jan Strycker.

Reynier B. Van Giesen, the man of so many duties in Flatbush, moved to Bergen where he died in 1707. He had five sons and three daughters. The sons were: 1. Bastien; 2. Abraham, born November 13, 1666; 3. Isaac; 4. Johannis; 5. Jacob, baptized 1670. Bastien and Abraham Van Giesen were the two brothers who settled within the jurisdiction of Newark.

There is a betrothal record in the Dutch Church at Bergen as follows:

Bastien Van Giesen, living at Achquechnonk, and Aeltje Hendrichx, living at Hackensack, both from Midwout, at Bergen, by Do. Tessemaker, June 10, 1688. M. June 25.

Bastien purchased land on the Passaic River between Second River and the Acquackanonk line. He was a deacon in the Acquackanonk church in 1694 and 1697, and an elder in 1700 and at various times until 1730. He died in 1751.

Abraham Van Giesen, who may have been the builder of the old stone house, was married at Bergen, October 25, 1691, to Fitje Andriesse from Communipaw, by

Voorlezer R. Van Giesen, before the Congregation, in the presence of the Court. He lived on a plantation within the present limits of Brookdale and Upper Montclair. His sons were: Rynier, Andries, Isaac, Abraham, and probably a Johannis who died before his father. He had four daughters; one of them, Prientje, born September 19, 1696, married Simeon Van Winkel; and it may be that the old stone house passed down through this line.

A number of years ago Lewis Cockefair tore down a house that stood well back from the road on the south side of Broad Street, not far from the Brookdale Baptist Church, that was known as the Van Giesen house. The foundations had the letters A. V. G. and date 1711 or 1714 marked at one end of the house, and 1727 at the other end. Abraham Garrabrant owned this property when he died in 1805.

Abraham Van Giesen died July 19, 1753, and his will directed that his estate on Third River be divided into two parts, Andries to have the north side, and Isaac the south side; other land was also divided among his sons, including 500 acres in Morris County. This latter may have been the "Van Giesen Purchase" which is believed to have been located at Horse Neck, now Fairfield.

During the Revolution one of the Van Giesens of Stone House Plains believed in being loyal to King George, and he showed it by joining the British army in September, 1777. He was another Abraham Van Giesen, and his home was on the west side of Broad Street, north of the present line of Watchung Avenue. In March, 1779, the State of New Jersey seized and sold this property under an act of confiscation passed December 11, 1778. The commissioners gave a deed to

Thomas Sigler, in consideration of three hundred pounds, that being the highest bid. This deed has been kept by the descendants of Thomas Sigler. The excavation which formed the cellar of the old house, and the old well on this property, were filled up a few years ago by Mr. Davidson. The house itself had disappeared before the earliest recollection of Eunice Sigler who was born in 1808. It was some distance north of the present dwelling, No. 998 Broad Street.

The Cockefair Family

The first of the Cockefair family in America was Alexander, a Frenchman who came in 1657. Six years later he obtained a plantation in Bushwick, Long Island, now a portion of Brooklyn. At that time he was drum major of the militia. It may have been his fine military bearing and uniform, which are always so attractive to those who do not bear arms, or it may have been his personality, but in April, 1665, he paid a marriage fee of six guilders to the Flatbush church. The last mention of his name is in 1698, when he sold some meadow land in Bushwick. Although he signed his name "Alexander Cokcover" it is generally understood that the correct spelling of the name is "Coquefaire." There were a great many French people in the Dutch colony, a fact that is often overlooked. It has been estimated that in the time of Governor Peter Stuyvesant, he of the wooden leg, one-quarter of the population of New Amsterdam was French. A John Cockefair was living in New York in 1690.

Alexander Cockefair, undoubtedly a grandson of the dignified drum major, was the first of the family to settle at Stone House Plains. Just when he came has not been learned, but his eldest son, still another Alex ander, was baptized at the Acquackanonk church in 1721. He had also a son John, born May 6, 1735; and these two headed the main branches of the family, known as the Alexander line and the John line. There were two daughters, one married Jacob Phillips and the other John Lawrence. The Lawrence house is the old stone house on Watchung Avenue east of Broad Street.

The first Cockefair house at Stone House Plains stood on land now owned by Sylvanus Cockefair, between the present dwelling and the spring to the south. There is a well now in use that is said to have been within the kitchen of the first house. Thomas Cockefair, who was born in 1762, knew of this old house but said it had disappeared before his earliest recollections.

The first Cockefair farm is supposed to have run from a ledge of rock in a field east of Broad Street, later owned by the Lindenmeyers, to an oak tree near the corner of Broad Street and Watchung Avenue; the eastern boundary being a line about 800 feet west of the Third River, and probably the present line of Broad Street on the west.

This farm was divided from time to time between sons and daughters. In 1753 the second Alexander of Stone House Plains added to his portion by a purchase which extended the farm to the Third River. The deed for this land is dated May 14th, the 27th year of King George II, and calls for forty-one acres. During the Revolutionary War this second Alexander's eldest son Zebulon, a boy of eighteen, was carried off from his home by the British soldiers when they were marching south through Stone House Plains, on their way back from the vicinity of Great Falls. His parents never saw him again, but they received word some time later that he had died on one of the prison ships. The road of that day lay several hundred feet east of the present line of Broad Street. It connected at the south with what is now Morris Place.

Isaac Cockefair, a grandson of the second Alexander, of Stone House Plains, abandoned the dwelling of his father and grandfather when William Parsons built him a new house in 1849. This house and land passed through various hands after the death of Isaac until 1911, when they were purchased by the Country Club of Glen Ridge. It was then known as the Jackson farm. The older house stood a few feet to the northeast of the present one. The excavation which formed the cellar of this old house of Colonial days was filled up in 1911.

At Wyoming in Pennsylvania near the present city of Wilkes Barre, one of the horrors of the Revolution was enacted. During the massacre two young girls hid behind a log while the Indians killed all the other members of their family. These girls were Mary and Naomi Hendershott, twin sisters eleven years old, and they succeeded in escaping with a few others to the settlements on the Delaware River. This was in July, 1778. Just when they came to Bloomfield is not known, but Thomas Cockefair, grandfather of Lewis, married Mary Hendershott, and a John Cockefair married Naomi. Mary lived until 1808, and Naomi until 1835.

The home of the latter, who was known as "Aunt Nomie," stood a few feet north of the present dwelling of John Henry Cockefair, 741 Broad Street. A depression in the ground shows where the cellar was excavated. The oldest Cockefair house now standing is the rear portion of 901 Broad Street. It belonged to the John Cockefair side of the family, and the date of its erection is not known. On one side the pitch of the roof has been changed in recent years to increase the head room of the attic. The larger portion of the house, facing Broad Street, was built by John Cockefair in 1817. This John was a son of Thomas Cockefair and Mary Hendershott, not the John who married Naomi. The road of Colonial days is supposed to have been on the opposite side of this house from the present Broad Street.

The Speer Family

Hendrick Jansen Spier emigrated from Amsterdam to America with his wife Madeline Hanse and two children, on the Dutch West India ship "Faith," arriving at New Amsterdam in December, 1659.

February 14, 1660, he bought a lot in New Amsterdam from Pieter Pieterse Menist. It was on the west side of Broad Street, about 300 feet north of Stone Street. In the spring of 1668 he removed to Bergen, buying of Jan Lubbertsen a tract of twenty-five morgen (fifty acres) near Communipaw. Governor Carteret confirmed the possession of this land to Spier by a patent of May 12, 1668. This property remained in the family till May 1, 1768. He died prior to 1680, and his widow married, December 16, 1681, Aertsen Van der Bilt, she being his third wife.

Hendrick Jansen Spier had three sons, the eldest, John Hendrick Spier, who was one of the company of fourteen who obtained the Acquackanonk patent; second, Barent Hendrick Spier, who remained at Communipaw; and third, Hans Hendrick Spier, who settled at Second River, and it was his son Hendrick, baptized October 5, 1685, who was, as far as we know, the first Dutch child born there.

John Hendrick Spier of Acquackanonk received, among other grants, a farm of two hundred acres on the Passaic River between Passaic and Delawanna, where he built a house of stone. He was married to Maria Franse at Bergen, August 12, 1679. The date of the first settlement at Acquackanonk can be closely approximated from the following facts. Franz, the second son of John Hendrick, was baptized April 2, 1683, and when he was married to Diercktie Corneliese at Hackensack March, 1705, it was recorded that both he and she were born at Acquackanonk. Like his cousin at Second River, Franz Spier may have been the first white child born in Acquackanonk. John Hendrick Spier's will was dated October 22, 1722, and proved September 18, 1724. A copy was obtained from Trenton, but it is too long to be inserted here. After providing for his wife, sons and daughters in the matter of real and personal estate, he seems greatly concerned about the brewing kettle; he says, "as for the Brew cettle and other yousful necessarys belonging to bruing it shall remain where it is for the aforesaid France and Jacob, but if any of the aforesaid children have a mind to brue in the said cettle they shall have the use thereof anything contrary to the true intent and meaning hereof notwithstanding."

A wife, three sons and seven daughters survived him, the sons were: Hendrick, Frans and Jacob. Jacob Spier married Lea Coejeman, December 5, 1746, and had three sons and three daughters. One of these sons, Hendrick, born in 1750, married Jannetje Van Giesen and had a daughter Elizabeth who married Starr Parsons.

Johannis Spier, a grandson of Hans Hendrick Spier,

the early settler at Second River, lived on the River road at Belleville. During the Revolution a man believed to be a British spy appeared on the opposite side of the Passaic River and called to be ferried across. Johannis refused, then taking his trusty flint-lock musket he climbed the steeple of the Dutch Church. From there he shot the man dead. A watch taken from his body is still in the possession of the family in Belleville. The distance from the old church to the opposite bank of the river scales on the map over two hundred yards.

Passaic County was organized by an Act of February 7, 1837. Before that time Acquackanonk was part of Essex County. Where the county line crosses East Passaic Avenue there is a boundary stone marked as follows:

(South:)	(East:)	(North:)
E. C.	1837	P. C.
Com.	J. R. Speer	C. G. Van Riper
P. Speer	Surv.	P. G. Speer
A. V. Speer		

Surely C. G. Van Riper's wife or mother must have been a Speer or he would not have been admitted to this family party.

THE GARRABRANT FAMILY

The first Garrabrants at Stone House Plains were two brothers, Garrabrant Garrabrant and Teunis Garrabrant. They were sons of Cornelius Garrabrant, and grandsons of Gerbrandt Cleasen and his wife Marritje Claes, who lived at Communipaw. His wife was a daughter of Claes Pietersen Coes. Gerbrandt Cleasen signed his will March 16, 1696-7, and it was proved April 22, 1708.

Garrabrant Garrabrant was born September 10, 1723, and married Catrina Pier; Teunis Garrabrant was born April 8, 1726, and died May 15, 1760; they had other brothers and sisters.

Garrabrant Garrabrant and Catrina Pier had three children: Garrabrant, born March 21, 1755; Jannetje, born March 1, 1760; and Cornelius, born February 18, 1765.

Abraham Garrabrant of a later generation, who married Elinor Kingsland, came into possession of a part of the Abraham Van Giesen estate, including the house with the cornerstone marked A. V. G. He died in 1805. The present investigation has brought to light a map of his property.

The Sigler Family

The first of the Siglers whose name has appeared in the present research was Daniel Sigler who lived at Second River, but who moved to Somerset County some time before his death in 1754. Mr. Davidson has a certified copy of his will written in the quaint old way on parchment. Among his personal effects his High Dutch Books were left to his daughter Catherine Hoffman. Was she able to read them?

He owned thirty acres of woodland on the Third River (the present poorhouse farm and the farm south of it) which he left to his son Henry. Henry Sigler settled on his inheritance and his home faced the stream. This house was torn down about the time that the present poorhouse was built. To his younger son, James, Daniel Sigler willed the homestead at Second River.

Thomas Sigler, another son of Daniel, was probably the first of the family to live at Stone House Plains.

There is extant an old book showing that he was a farmer and had had an account against John Cockefair in August, 1860, for "rie," "weet," turnips, oats, carting, etc. Lewis Cockefair remembers a stone house on Broad street, at the corner of Watchung Avenue, that had the date 1741 over the door, and it was known as the Sigler house.

There is a stone in the foundation of the house now on the site of the Sigler house marked with a heart, the letters C. F. I. and 1774. The letters stand for Christopher and Frouchey Interest. This stone has been in its present position but a few years. There is some difference of opinion as to the original location of these stones bearing the dates 1741 and 1774. There is a memorandum in an old book which says "Elizabeth Interest was born Sept. 2nd, 1774." She has been gone these many years, but the stone with the heart and the date are still to be seen. She married Moses Sigler (a son of Thomas who bought the confiscated homestead of Abraham Van Giesen) and they had eleven children.

An old bill of sale recalls Elizabeth Interest. Moses Sigler, her husband, having died in 1825, she was called "Widow Betsy Sigler." In September, 1830, the Widow Betsy sold to Jabez Cook her slave woman Zilpha. The interesting feature of the sale is that the slave had run away, and part of the purchase money was contingent upon her being found within ninety days.

After the battle of Long Island, August, 1776, Washington retreated slowly and crossed the Passaic River at Acquackanonk, coming from Hackensack. This was November 21st, and on the 23d he was in Newark. His army was reduced to about 3,500 men. Probably most of the men marched to Newark by the river road, but some of them came through Stone House Plains. The officers halted and stayed a short time at the stone house by the Oak Tree, the Sigler house.

In 1780 William Herne, Quartermaster, gave Christopher Interest a receipt for two bushels of Indian corn for the use of the 1st Brigade of Infantry, Commanded by General Hand. The fact that this receipt is still preserved indicates that Christopher was never paid for the Indian corn.

The Cueman Family

The Coejeman, or Cueman, family was in Brookdale at an early date. The will of Lukas Cowman of Newark, dated August 7, 1712, and proved February 12, 1717-8, mentions, wife Ariantie; children Jacob, Johannis; Mary, wife of Cornelius Tomason; Yonitie, wife of Gidion van Winkle; five children of daughter Geartie, deceased; also real and personal property.

There is also a record of the sale of forty acres of upland on the plain beyond Mill River by Hance Alberts to Hendrick, Jacob and Johannis Cueman, November 18, 1699. This may not have been the first land in Brookdale purchased by the Cueman family, and it is possible that Luke Cueman built the old stone house, and that it passed to the Van Wagoners through his daughter Yonitie (Jannitie) who married Gidion Symese van Winkle March 13, 1708. The marriage record at Hackensack says that Jannetie was born at Albany.

The Cueman farm of recent years adjoined the farm on which the old stone house stands.

AN AFTERNOON WALK

By Maud Parsons

As one strolls northward through Brookdale from the end of the trolley the first place of historic interest is the hill to the west. In 1856 this was the site of the Methodist Church that was later united with the Park Methodist Church.

To the east is the bed of what was once the Morris pond. This is now covered with a growth of underbrush where the first blue-birds and robins come in the spring, and where red-winged blackbirds are seen in great numbers in September. Mention of the pond brings to mind the old Morris mill which stood at the southwest corner of Bay Lane and Morris Place for nearly two hundred years, having been built in 1702. That site was where the mechanical parts for the Morris Canal were made by Ira Dodel and Caleb D. Baldwin, and was a scene of great activity about 1830.

In speaking of the canal, while it never has been of great use in the economic advancement of the little community, it has afforded the young people much pleasure. What boy who has ever lived in Brookdale will soon forget the good swimming at the "Rock"? And who can say that the existence of the canal is not justified by the good times it has brought to those—and they have been many—who have whizzed along on its glassy surface in winter? And as for canoeing, only the pen of a Stevenson could describe its charm.

But to come back to Broad Street and the bend in the road, from which place we can view one of the prettiest bits of landscape in North Jersey—an interesting landscape, as well. In the field to the right, not far from the stream, there used to be a large boulder which was the starting point for the surveys of the various farms in Stone House Plains. This was blasted out some few years ago by Henry Lindenmeyer. Then there is the brook beyond, a famous trout stream (so we judge from the number of fishermen seen along its banks on the first of April). But the most welcome sight, if the day be hot, is the row of tall maples fronting the Lindenmeyer estate. A few years back there was a similar row on the other side of the road, but these were cut down when the road was widened, probably to accommodate the long-hoped-for trolley extension. If you are a lover of birds, before going farther look into the evergreens on the side of the hill for blue jays, for that is their rendezvous; and in the woods across the pond you may see a kingfisher. Or if the fragrant julep is your idea of refreshment, lean over the fence for a bit of the fresh scented mint that grows around the spring.

If you are interested in golf, the new links of the Country Club will probably prove so attractive that you will wish to go no farther.

If not, the next spot of interest is the old cemetery which has been neglected for many years, and offers an excellent opportunity for some improvement society to do good work. Myrtle has grown wild there, and covers the ground in almost a solid mass. At the expense of very little time and trouble this could be made a spot truly delightful to the eye. The sandstone headstones with their quaint legends, and old-fashioned long s's, are extremely interesting and well worth preserving.

One bears the date of 1788, while there are two dates 1804 and one 1808.

On the lot in front of this graveyard stood the oldest known schoolhouse in Stone House Plains, and Starr Parsons, who came from Redding, Connecticut, is thought to have been the first schoolmaster. This school was burned in December, 1835. A new school was not built until twelve years later, and in 1857 the new school was replaced by what is now the old Brookdale school.

Before the Brookdale school system was incorporated with that of Bloomfield, this little red brick building was a typical country school where there were pieces to speak and spelling matches on Friday afternoons. And those democratic old double seats were a real joy in more ways than one. For instance, every day the teacher would write twenty words on the board for that day's spelling lesson. You would learn the first ten, your seat mate the last, and by combining your efforts each have a perfect paper. This in a spirit, not of dishonesty, but of mutual helpfulness and economy—call it conservation of energy, if you will.

In the winter, when skating was good, the great majority of the pupils spent the noon hour on the canal. They were too far away to hear the sound of the bell, which was of the ordinary dinner variety; so when tardiness became too prevalent a compromise was hit upon whereby the teacher was to hang out a red shawl at ten minutes of one. What good games of "shinney" and bantry and "snap-the-whip" did that old shawl end.

In the house beyond the school, at present occupied by Bloomfield Howland, lived Simeon Brown, a man who was evidently very proud of his fine handwriting.

The Rev. Joseph F. Folsom of Newark picked up an old book in a local bookstore one day last year. It was "A Treatise on the Jurisdiction and Proceedings of Justices of the Peace in Civil Suits in New Jersey" (Simeon, by the way, was Justice of the Peace), printed in Burlington in 1813. These were the stanzas he found in the book, both written out "plain" and "neat":

> This is my Book, as you may Know,
> By Letters Plain I will it Show:
> The first is S., a Letter Bright,
> The next is B., in all men's Sight:
> And if you chance to read amiss,
> Look under neat and there it is.
> SIMEON BROWN.

December 9, 1816.

> Simeon Brown is my Name,
> Stone House Plains is my station,
> Heaven is my Dwelling Place,
> And Christ is my salvation;
> When I am Dead and in my Grave,
> And all my Bones are Rotten,
> This you may see to Remember me,
> That I am not Forgotten.

December 9, 1816.

BOARD OF TRADE CENTENNIAL RESOLUTION

At the last meeting of the executive committee of the Board of Trade a sub-committee was appointed to obtain information concerning the setting off of the township of Bloomfield from the township of Newark in 1812, with instructions to report to the executive committee at this meeting. In accordance with those instructions the committee submits the following report:

Newark was settled by some thirty families of Puritans who came from Connecticut in May, 1666. The arrangements for the settlement were made with the representative of the Lord Proprietors of New Jersey, Lord John Berkely and Sir George Carteret, to whom the province had been granted by James, Duke of York. After some trouble with the Indians a purchase was made from them which included the territory afterward known as Bloomfield, and this latter territory was gradually settled by farmers from the Newark settlement and by the Dutch who came in from Bergen County on the northeast.

For one hundred and forty years there were no subdivisions of Newark, but in 1806 three wards were established known as the Newark Ward, Orange Ward and Bloomfield Ward. This division determined the southern boundary of Bloomfield.

On January 24, 1812, the Council and General Assembly of New Jersey passed an act setting off a new township from the township of Newark and incorporated it by the name of "The Inhabitants of the township of Bloomfield in the county of Essex." The act provided, however, that it should not be in force until the fourth Monday of March (March 23), 1812. That day, therefore, was the beginning of Bloomfield as a municipality, and three weeks later the first town meeting was held at the house of Isaac Ward. Unfortunately, all records of the early meetings of the township have been lost, the only old record in the office of the town clerk being a cash book which was started in 1812. A copy of the act setting off Bloomfield from Newark is annexed to this report.

The area of the original township of Bloomfield was about twenty and a half square miles, and it was bounded on the north by the Passaic County line; on the east by the Passaic River; on the south by the townships of Newark and Orange, and on the west by the crest of First Mountain. This district included the present municipalities of Bloomfield, Glen Ridge, Montclair, Nutley and Belleville, and a part of what is now the Forest Hill and Woodside section of Newark. In 1820 this territory had a population of 3,085.

BLOOMFIELD, OLD AND NEW

Although Bloomfield had no separate existence until 1812, the name had been adopted some years earlier. The Presbyterian Church was started in 1794, and in 1796 the congregation worshiping in the Joseph Davis house on Franklin Street, adopted the name of Bloomfield for their community, and for the church which was organized in that year. When the edifice at the head of the Green was erected, a tablet with the inscription "Bloomfield 1796" was placed in the tower.

The name was taken in honor of General Joseph Bloomfield, who was a distinguished citizen of New Jersey. General Bloomfield had served in the War of the Revolution as a captain, and afterward major of New Jersey regulars from 1775 to 1778. From 1783 to 1788 he was Attorney-General of New Jersey, and in 1794 was a brigadier-general of New Jersey militia, commanding troops during the "Whiskey Rebellion." From 1801 to 1802 and 1803 to 1812, he was Governor of New Jersey, and *ex-officio* Chancellor of the State. Governor Bloomfield relinquished his office on March 27, 1812, four days after the township of Bloomfield was formed, to become a brigadier-general of regulars in the United States Army, commanding the third military district with headquarters at New York City. After the War of 1812 was over he rounded out his career as a representative from New Jersey in the Congress of the United States. It is evident that when the members of the old First Church were choosing a name for their community in 1796, they settled upon a man whose later achievements fully confirmed their estimate of him. Bloomfield may well be proud of its name.

This committee believes that Bloomfield's centennial should be celebrated next year in a suitable manner, and that such a celebration will be of great benefit to the town. The Board of Trade is unquestionably the proper body to undertake this work, and the committee recommends that steps be taken in the near future to bring the matter to the attention of the Board of Trade and the people of Bloomfield with this end in view.

        RANDOLPH C. BARRETT, *Chairman*.
        HOWARD B. DAVIS.
        WILLIAM BIGGART.

Bloomfield, N. J., May 4, 1911.

ACT OF INCORPORATION IN 1812

AN ACT TO SET OFF AND ERECT A NEW TOWNSHIP FROM THE TOWNSHIP OF NEWARK, IN THE COUNTY OF ESSEX.

SEC. 1. *Be it enacted* by the council and general assembly of this State, and it is hereby enacted by the authority of the same, That all the district of the township of Newark in the county of Essex, included within the following limits, viz.: Beginning at the Green island in Passaic River near that part of the road leading from Newark to Belleville called the gully, and from thence running westerly to the northeast corner of the township of Orange at the great boiling spring, thence along the line of the township of Orange to Turkey-Eagle rock on the top of the first mountain, thence northerly along the said Orange line on the top of said mountain to the corner of the township of Caldwell, thence along the Caldwell line on the top of said mountain to the line of the township of Acquacknonk, thence southeasterly along the said Acquacknonk line to Passaic River, thence southerly along said Passaic River to the beginning, be, and the same is hereby set off from the said township of Newark, and erected into a separate township, to be known by the name of the township of Bloomfield.

2. *And be it enacted,* That the inhabitants of said township of Bloomfield shall be and they are hereby vested with and entitled to all the powers, privileges and authorities, and shall be and are hereby made subject to the like regulations and government which the inhabitants of other townships in this State are subject and entitled to, and that the inhabitants of the township of Bloomfield shall be and they are hereby incorporated, styled and known by the name of "The inhabitants of the township of Bloomfield in the county of Essex," and entitled to all the privileges, authorities and advantages that the other townships in the said county are entitled to by virtue of an act entitled "An act incorporating the inhabitants of townships, designating their powers and regulating their meetings," passed the twenty-first day of February in the year of our Lord one thousand seven hundred and ninety-eight, *Provided,* that this act shall not be in force until the fourth Monday of March next.

3. *And be it enacted,* That the inhabitants of the said township of Bloomfield shall hold their first town-meeting at the house where Isaac Ward now dwells, on the day appointed by law for holding the annual town-meetings in the other townships in the county of Essex.

4. *And be it enacted,* That every person becoming chargeable as a pauper after the first day of November, eighteen hundred and eleven, shall be supported after the fourth Monday of March next by the township within the limits of which he or she may have gained his or her last residence, and that the township committees of Newark and Bloomfield shall meet on the Monday next after the town-meetings in said townships, at the house of Moses Roff in the town of Newark, at ten o'clock in the forenoon, and then and there proceed to make an allotment between the said townships of such poor persons as shall have been chargeable on the first day of November aforesaid, in proportion to the taxable property and ratables as taxed by the assessor within their respective limits, to be ascertained by the duplicate of the present year, and that said township of Bloomfield shall be entitled to receive from the township of Newark their proportion of all moneys on hand or due, arising from taxes, and also one hundred and forty-two dollars and eighty-five cents, the proportion of money expended in defending the town lands, and shall be liable to pay their proportion of the debts if any there should be at the time, and if either of the above mentioned committees or parts of said committees shall neglect or refuse to meet as aforesaid, it shall and may be lawful for such members of the said committees as do meet to proceed to such allotment of poor, the distribution of property and debts, which shall be conclusive and final.

A. Passed at Trenton, January 24, 1812.
(Act of 1812, 36th Ses. 3d Sit., p. 62.)
NOTE.—The fourth Monday in March, 1812, was March 23d.

Town meetings in the various townships of Essex County were held on the second Monday in April in each year. (Act of 1798, 22d Ses., 2d Sit., p. 289, Sec. 3.)

CENTENNIAL CELEBRATION

BLOOMFIELD, NEW JERSEY

June 9, 10, 11, 12, 13, 1912

EXECUTIVE COMMITTEE OF BOARD OF TRADE

Hon. Amzi Dodd,
Honorary Chairman.
Frederick M. Davis,
Chairman.
Eugene L. R. Cadmus,
Secretary.
Howard B. Davis,
Treasurer.
Matthew McCrodden,
Allison Dodd,
Randolph C. Barrett,
David G. Garabrant,
Theodore H. Ward,
Henry Albinson,
Benjamin Haskell,
William A. Baldwin,
Charles Ferguson,
William P. Sutphen,

Lewis B. Harrison,
Mayor William Hauser,
David Oakes,
Alfred H. Edgerley,
Edward J. Hughes,
George Morris,
Charles A. Hungerford,
Herbert C. Farrand,
George Hummel,
Charles J. Murray,
William Biggart,
William H. Hays,
Frank N. Unangst,
Frederick Sadler,
Walter Ellor,
Harry L. Osborne,
Theodore E. Jones.

On Saturday evening, March 23, 1912, was held the first popular meeting of the centennial celebration. The citizens gathered at the Old First Church, and the following programme, arranged by the committee on public meetings, was carried out:

Organ prelude, Miss Laura P. Ward; Invocation, Rev. George L. Curtis, D.D.; Singing by the High School Glee Club, led by P. J. Smith; Introductory remarks, the Mayor, Hon. William Hauser; Reading of the 1812 Act of Incorporation, Frederick M. Davis; Address, Hon. John Franklin Fort, former Governor of New Jersey.

SUB-COMMITTEES OF THE CENTENNIAL CELEBRATION

BLOOMFIELD, NEW JERSEY
June 9, 10, 11, 12, 13, 1912

Finance Committee: Matthew McCrodden, *Chairman,* Allison Dodd, Harry L. Osborne, Arthur Russell, *Secretary,* James W. Crisp, Jr., F. J. Dahl, Albert W. Fish, Frank Foster, Charles H. Madole, Howard B. Davis.

Invitation and Reception: Randolph C. Barrett, *Chairman,* David G. Garabrant, Theodore H. Ward, Henry Albinson, Alfred B. Van Liew, Frank A. Stone, *Secretary.*

Historical: Benjamin Haskell, *Chairman,* William A. Baldwin, *Secretary,* Charles C. Ferguson, Rev. George L. Curtis, D.D., Rev. Joseph F. Folsom, William P. Sutphen, Raymond F. Davis.

Public Meeting (Tuesday, June 11th) and Historical Exhibit: William P. Sutphen, *Chairman,* Lewis B. Harrison, F. R. Hinkle, George Kerr, James E. Brooks, *Secretary.*

Industrial: Mayor Hauser, *Chairman,* David Oakes, Alfred H. Edgerley, Peter H. Fowler, R. H. Henderson, E. D. Farmer, Ralph Thompson, John M. Hague, *Secretary.*

Parade and Decoration: Ed. J. Hughes, *Chairman,* Eugene L. R. Cadmus, *Secretary,* Timothy P. Edwards, R. R. Johnson, J. R. Richardson, B. F. Higgins.

Educational (including school children parade): George Morris, *Chairman,* Charles A. Hungerford, Miss Jessie Colfax, *Secretary,* William S. S. Rowland. Sixty names added January 12th on file.

Banquet: Charles A. Hungerford, *Honorary Chairman;* Harry L. Osborne, *Active Chairman,* James W. Crisp, Jr., *Secretary.*

Music: Herbert C. Farrand, *Chairman,* George Hummel, Charles W. Martin, David P. Lyall, William J. Maier.

Fireworks: Charles J. Murray, *Chairman,* William Biggart, *Secretary,* Frank De Moyne, Joseph E. Garabrant, E. Thornton Rice.

Press Committee: William H. Hays, Frank N. Unangst.

Printing, Souvenir Programme and Badges: Frederick Sadler, *Chairman,* Walter Ellor, Howard B. Davis, Henry Albinson, Frank L. Fischer, Charles W. Havens, Frank B. Daley, Graham M. Johnstone, Raymond F. Davis.

Monument: David G. Garabrant, *Chairman,* William P. Sutphen, Theodore H. Ward, Charles A. Hungerford.

Folk Dances: Theodore H. Ward, *Chairman,* William S. Cannon, *Secretary,* Dr. H. E. Richards, Mrs. Elmer C. Robaud, Mrs. E. W. Baldwin, Mrs. H. R. Underwood, Mrs. A. B. Van Liew.

INDEX

Academy, Bloomfield, 14, 82.
Acquackanonk, 162, 163, 164, 169, 176, 186.
After the Revolution, 43.
An Afternoon Walk, 180.
Archdeacon's Hotel, 149.
Armstrong, Amzi, 81.

Baechlin, Ernest, 160.
Baldwin, Caleb, 30.
Baldwin Family, 15, 16.
Baldwin, Warren S., 16, 90, 92, 109, 146.
Baldwin, William A., 7, 78, 92.
Ball Family, 23.
Ball, Mark W., 10, 38.
Ballentine, Henry W., Rev., 120.
Band, brass, first, 63.
Baptist Church, First, 8, 124.
Barrett, Randolph C., 185, 189.
Belleville, 70, 141, 142, 166, 176.
Bergen Exploit, 37.
Berkeley School, 96.
Bibliography, Bloomfield, 8, 9.
Biggart, William, 185.
Black, Joseph, mill, 31.
Bloomfield, General Joseph, 45, 54, 119, 186.
Bloomfield Savings Inst., 146.
Bloomfield Township, 69, 70.
Board of Trade, 7, 153-155.
Boundaries of Newark, 11, 69, 185, 187.
Bradbury, William B., 93.
Brady's Mill, 2, 31.
Brewing kettle, 175.
"Brick pits," 53.
British Army, 170, 172.
British raids, 32, 172.
Broad Street, 172, 173, 174.
Brokaw, Joshua C., 80, 109.
Bromley, Dury, 31.
Brookdale, 163.
Brookdale Baptist Church, 135.
Brookdale Reformed Church, 122, 168, 169.
Brookdale schools, 85, 86, 169, 182.
Brooks, James E., 162.
Broughton, John G., 121.
Broughton Memorial, 121.
Brown, Simeon, 182.
Burying ground, 53.

Cadmus, Eugene L. R., 188.
Cadmus Family, 24.

Cadmus house, 25, 40.
Caldwell church, 52, 53.
Canal boats, 106.
Cannon, brass, 50, 51.
Canon, iron, 52.
Capen, John F., 10.
Captahen, 164.
Carteret, Sir George, 184.
Carteret, Philip, Governor, 28.
Catholic Lyceum, 134.
Cemetery, 53.
Central School, 80, 86, 87, 92.
Chancellor, William E., 9.
Chapman, Jedidiah, Rev., 41, 81.
Christ Episcopal Church, 127.
Church bell, 14.
Church manuals, 9.
Church of the Ascension, 137.
Churches of Bloomfield, 118.
"Citizen," Bloomfield, 9
Civil War, 64.
Civil War Veterans, 66.
Cockefair Family, 166, 171, 174.
Cockefair, Lewis, 9, 170, 178
Collins, Thomas, 42, 51, 63.
Combination Rubber Mfg. Co., 145.
Consolidated Safety Pin Co., 144.
Cooke, Harriet B., 82, 83.
Cooke, Robert L., 62, 82.
Copper mines, 26, 27.
Crab Orchard, 44.
Crane Family, 14.
Crane, Israel, 15, 55, 103.
Crane, I. W., letter, 45.
Crane, Jasper, mill, 31.
Cueman Family, 179.
Curtis, George L., 7, 118.

Davis, Charles M., 84, 91.
Davis Family, 18, 19, 88.
Davis, Fredk. M., 71, 188.
Davis, Howard B., 185, 188, 189.
Davis, Joseph, house, 18, 39, 47, 186.
Davis, Dr. J. A., 19, 37, 109.
Davis, Raymond F., 7, 69.
Deed for Green, 55.
Diamond Mills Paper Co., 145.
Dodd, Allison, 147, 158.
Dodd, Amzi, 9, 18, 46, 110.
Dodd, Daniel, 17, 167.
Dodd, Daniel, "1719 House," 17.
"Dominie, The," poem, 53.
Dodd Family, 17.
Dodd, Ira, 16, 110, 180.
Dodd, John, General, 18, 103.

INDEX

Dodd, Stephen, Rev., 8, 81.
Dodd, Zophar B., 62, 145.
Duffield, Samuel W., 158.
Dunbar, John B., 95.
Dutch families, 26.
Dutch names, 165.
Dutch Reformed ministers, 122, 123.

Eagle Rock, 187.
Elm trees, 62.
Episcopal ministers, 127, 128, 137, 138.
Empire Cream Separator Co., 145.
Essex County B. and L. Ass'n, 148.
Eucleian Society, 46, 152.
Executive Committee, 188.

Farrand house, 40.
Farrand, Herbert C., 189.
Farrand, Moses, 30, 40.
Female Seminary, 83.
Ferguson, Charles C., 7, 101.
Fire Department, 74, 75, 149.
First Baptist Church, 8, 124.
First Mountain, 28.
First Presbyterian Church, 46-53, 54, 118.
Folsom, Joseph F., 7, 11, 32, 43.
Ford, John, Rev., 82.
Fordham, Stephen, 52.
Fort, John Franklin, Hon., 188.
Franklin (Watsesson) Hill, 39.
Franklin incorporated, 72.
Franklin school-house, 78, 81.
Franklin stove, 85.
Fraternities, 152.
Frazer, D. R., Rev., 139
Free schools, 84, 88, 89.

Garabrant, David G. S., 8, 189.
Garabrant Family, 176, 177.
Garret, Garretson, 165.
Gas lighting, 75.
Graveyard, Brookdale, 181.
German Presbyterian church, 125.
German Theological Seminary, 82, 139.
Gibb, James, 58, 62.
Gildersleeve, Cyrus, Rev., 50, 61.
Glen Ridge Congregational Church, 135.
Glen Ridge incorporated, 72.
Glenwood Avenue station, 110, 158.
Green, Jacob, Rev., 49.
Green, The, 8, 20, 54.
Greenwood Lake Railroad, 111, 143.
Grist mills, 141.
Grover, Joseph, Rev., 49.
Gwinn, William, mill, 30.

Hall, Eliphalet, 57, 62.
Harrison, Caleb, well, 31.

Harrison, George, mill, 30.
Hartman, Michaelsen, 164.
Haskell, Benjamin, 7, 23.
Hauser, William, Mayor, 77, 188.
Hays, William H., 189
Hendershott, Mary and Naomie, 173.
High School, 93-95, 98.
Historical Committee, 7.
Hulin, Stephen M., 8.
Home Lots, Newark, 11, 12.
Hooglandt, Christopher, 164.
Hope Chapel, 121.
Horse car railroads, 112.
Horse Neck, 28, 170.
Hoyt's "Orange Church," 37.
Hughes, Edward J., 189.
Hungerford, Charles A., 189.

Incorporation Act, 69, 186.
Indians, New Jersey, 12, 27, 28, 29, 162, 164.
Indian trail, 15.
Inhabitants of 1796, 43.
Inhabitants of 1830, 61.
Interest, Christopher, 178.

Jackson, Abel, Rev., 48, 49.
Jarvie, James N., 130, 147, 153.
Jarvie Memorial Library, 130, 153.
Jones, Charles G., 98.

Kettle, historic, 46.
Kidney, Captain John, 37.
King, Aury, 53, 54.
King, Mrs. John, 34.
Kinsey, Charles, 57.
Kocher, C. F., 160.
Knox, Charles E., Rev., 8, 9, 19.

Lackawanna Railroad, 158, 159.
Lawrence, John, 172.
Lecture room, 120.
Lewis, Amzi, Rev., 49, 81, 82.
Lindenmeyer, Henry, 181.
Lodges, 152.
Lutheran Church, 136.

McCrodden, Matthew, 189.
McCullough, George, 105.
McMichael, Captain, 38.
Madrigal Society, 153.
Mammoth bones, 57.
Maps of the village, 43, 61.
Meade, J. K., 57.
Merchant, Silas, 85.
Methodist Episcopal ministers, 123, 124, 132.
Mills of Bloomfield, 16, 140, 141.
Ministers, Presbyterian, 119, 126, 129, 130.
Montclair incorporated, 72.
Montclair, 14, 72.
Montgomery Chapel, 131.
Morris and Essex Railroad, 108, 158.

INDEX

iii

Morris Canal, 16, 104, 141.
Morris County Associate Presbytery, 48, 52.
Morris deed, 22.
Morris, Ephraim, 47, 60, 105, 119, 163.
Morris Family, 21, 23.
Morris, George, 189.
Morris mill, 25, 140, 180.
Morris Neighborhood, 15, 16, 80, 140.
Murray, Charles J., 189.

Names of Bloomfield localities, 44, 69, 70, 163.
Naming Bloomfield, 44.
Nardiello, Joseph M., Rev., 133.
Nelson, William, 9, 35, 166.
Newark and Bloomfield R. R., 109, 142.
Newark settlers, 13, 133, 140.
New Jersey Volunteers, 64.
Newtown road, 33, 37.

Oakes, David, 109.
Oakes, John, 10, 54.
Oakes Mill, 143.
Oakes, Thomas, 31, 51.
Oakes, Thomas, Second, 91, 92.
Oak Tree Lane, 172, 179.
Occupations of Inhabitants, 61.
Ogden, Captain John, 19, 80.
Old Road, Bloomfield, 15, 43, 102.
Orange and Bloomfield horse cars, 113.
Orange incorporated, 69.
Organization of First Church, 47.
Osborne, Harry L., 189.

Park Methodist Episcopal Church, 123, 180.
Park System, 157.
Parochial school, 95.
Parsons, Starr, 85, 182.
Parsons, Maud, 180.
Parsons, William, 173.
Paterson, 164.
Peeletown, 143.
Perine, H. M., Rev., 82, also map.
Peters, William K., 20.
Piano, first, 63.
Pier, Tunis Jansen, 166, 167.
Pilch, Frederick R., 91, 92.
Plum, Samuel, 167.
Poor House, 177.
Presbyterian ministers, 49, 119, 126, 129, 130.
Presbytery of New York, 47.
Public Records Commission, 35.

Quarries, 25, 54, 114.

Railroad service, 114.
Randolph, Hugh F., mill, 29, 30.
Randolph, Jacob F., 106.
Revolutionary Claims, 36.

Revolutionary Period, 32, 176, 178.
Revolutionary Veterans, 42.
Riots, Essex County, 27, 28.
Roads, 25, 102, 103.
Roman Catholics, 133, 137.
Root, J. H., 95.

Sacred Heart, Church of, 133.
Sadler, Frederick, 189
St. John's Evang. Lutheran, 136.
St. Valentine's R. C. Church, 137.
School Act of 1849, 84.
School bell "1776," 79.
School-house on the Green, 56, 80.
School principals, 89.
Schools, 78.
School trustees, 89, 90.
Scott and Bowne, 145.
Scott's Emulsion, 145.
Second River, 11, 15.
Sergeant, Isaac, 81.
Sewer system, 75, 151.
Seymour, Ebenezer, Rev., 84.
Sherman, John, 92.
Sherwood, James E., Rev., 8.
Seymour, Philander, 81.
Shields, James, 81.
Sigler Family, 177-179.
Silver Lake Chapel, 124.
Speer Family, 166, 174-176.
Spier, John Hendrick, 174.
Sprague Elevator Co., 145.
Stone House, The old, 167.
Stonehouse Brook, 167, 168.
Stone House Plain, 84, 85, 122, 162.
Stone houses, 25.
Stryker, Peter, Rev., 122.
Superstitions, 56.
Sutphen, William P., 7, 77, 140.

Third River, 11, 16, 162, 166, 167.
Thomas, M. D., 81.
Toney's Brook, 15, 54.
Town Act of 1900, 76.
Town Improvement Ass'n, 161.
Town officials, 71-74, 77.
Township of Bloomfield, 69, 70.
Transportation, 101.
Trust Company, 147.
Turnpike, Newark and Pompton, 101, 103.

Underwood, Charles R., 158.
Union School, 80.
Urian, Thomassen, 165.

Van Blarcom Family, 165.
Van Dyck's chocolate mill, 30.
Van Giesen Family, 168, 169-171.
Van Giesen Purchase, 164.
Van Houten Family, 166.
Van Liew, A. B., 160.
Van Riper Family, 165.
Van Wagener Family, 165.
Van Wagener, Garret, 168.

iv INDEX

Van Winkle Family, 165, 168.
Vreeland Family, 165.
Wakely house, 38.
Washington in Bloomfield, 40, 178.
Ward Family, 20, 167.
Ward, Jacob, 20-35.
Ward, Theodore H., 189.
Ward's Lane, 20, 26.
Wardsesson, 36, 43, 44.
Watchung Avenue, 170, 178.
Water system, 75, 137, 149, 150.
Watsessing dock, 102.
Watsessing M. E. Church, 132.
Watsesson Hill, 15, 47.

Watsesson Plain, 15, 24, 31, 32.
Wayne, General, 40.
Westervelt Family, 165.
Westinghouse Lamp Co., 145.
Westminster Presbyterian Church, 129.
White, William H., M.D., 146, 147.
Wiggins, H. B., Son Co., 145.
Wilson, Alexander, 27, 49, 55-60.
Winne house, 25, 33, 37.
Witchcraft, 56.
Woodside incorporated, 72.

Yantecaw River, 162, 163.

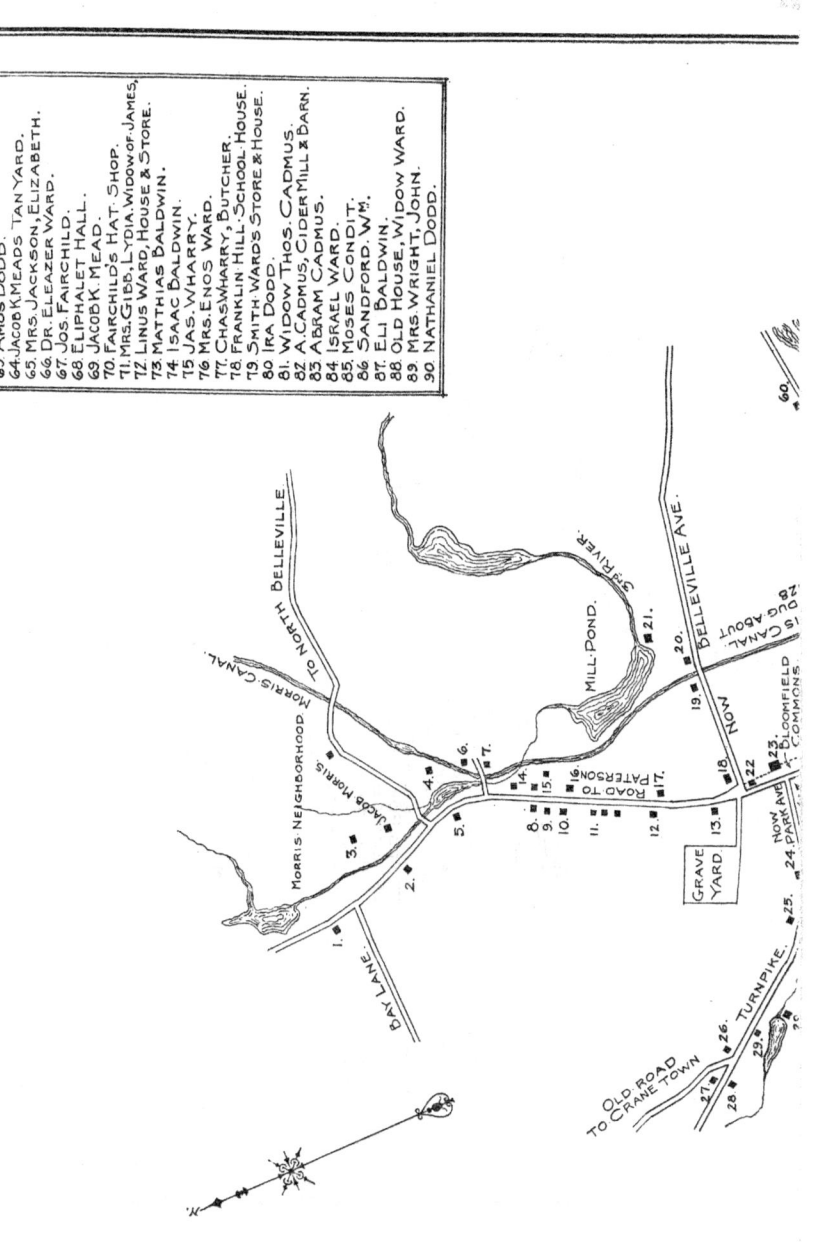

63. AMOS DODD.
64. JACOB K MEADS TAN YARD.
65. MRS. JACKSON, ELIZABETH.
66. DR. ELEAZER WARD.
67. JOS. FAIRCHILD.
68. ELIPHALET HALL.
69. JACOB K. MEAD.
70. FAIRCHILD'S HAT. SHOP.
71. MRS. GIBB, LYDIA. WIDOW OF JAMES,
72. LINUS WARD, HOUSE & STORE.
73. MATTHIAS BALDWIN.
74. ISAAC BALDWIN.
75. JAS. WHARRY.
76. MRS. ENOS WARD.
77. CHAS. WHARRY, BUTCHER.
78. FRANKLIN HILL. SCHOOL. HOUSE.
79. SMITH WARDS STORE & HOUSE.
80. IRA DODD.
81. WIDOW THOS. CADMUS.
82. A. CADMUS, CIDER MILL & BARN.
83. ABRAM CADMUS.
84. ISRAEL WARD.
85. MOSES CONDIT.
86. SANDFORD. WM.
87. ELI BALDWIN.
88. OLD HOUSE, WIDOW WARD.
89. MRS. WRIGHT, JOHN.
90. NATHANIEL DODD.

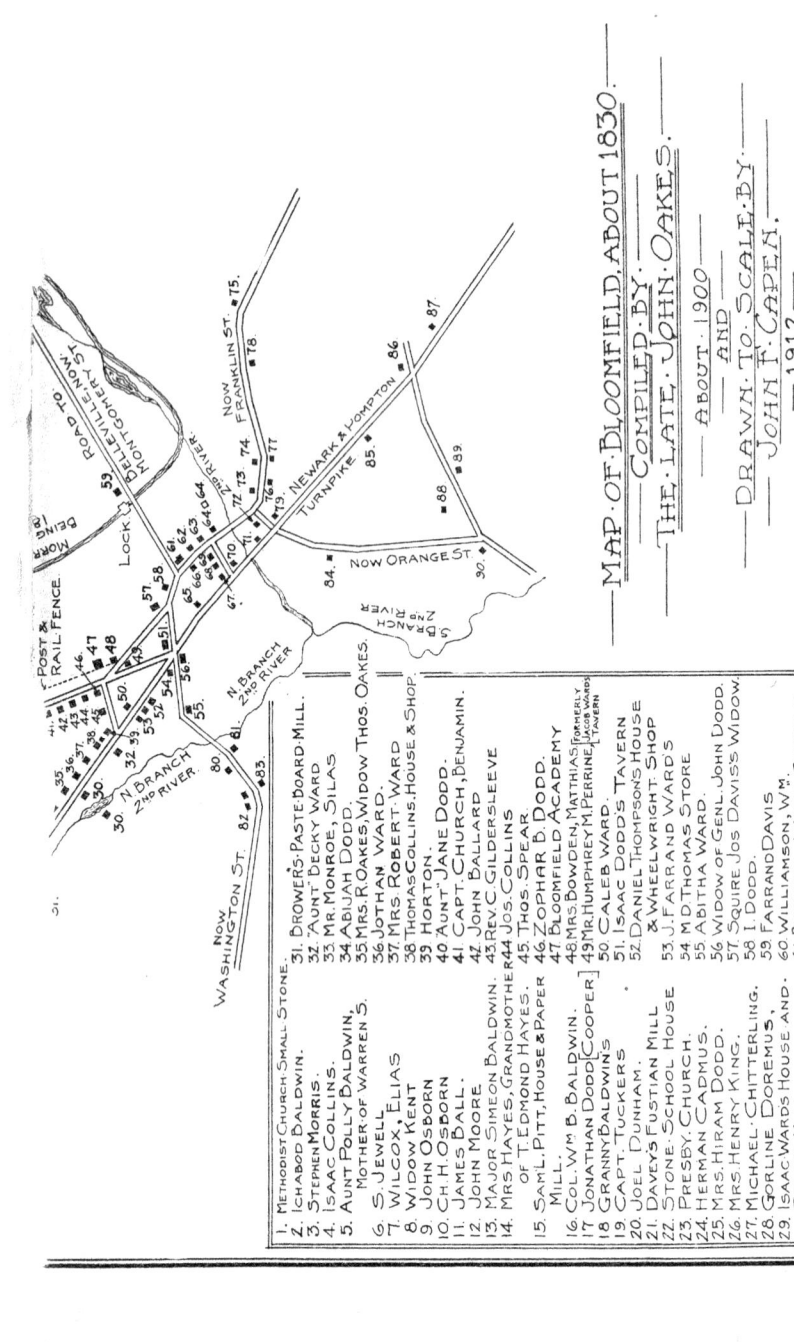

www.ingramcontent.com/pod-product-compliance
Lightning Source LLC
Chambersburg PA
CBHW071715160426
43195CB00012B/1689